EXCEL 2022

The Complete Illustrative Guide for Beginners to **Learning** any Fundamental, Formula, Function and **Chart in Less than 5 Minutes** with Simple and Real-Life Examples

Nigel Tillery

© Copyright 2022 by NIGEL TILLERY—All rights reserved.

This document is geared towards providing exact and reliable information regarding the topic and issue covered. The publication is sold with the idea that the publisher is not required to render accounting, officially permitted, or otherwise, qualified services. If advice is necessary, legal, or professional, a practiced individual in the profession should be ordered.

From a Declaration of Principles which was accepted and approved equally by a Committee of the American Bar Association and a Committee of Publishers and Associations.

In no way is it legal to reproduce, duplicate, or transmit any part of this document in either electronic means or printed format. Recording of this publication is strictly prohibited, and any storage of this document is not allowed unless with written permission from the publisher. All rights reserved.

The information provided here is stated to be truthful and consistent, in that any liability, in terms of inattention or otherwise, by any usage or abuse of any policies, processes, or directions contained within is the solitary and utter responsibility of the recipient reader. Under no circumstances will any legal responsibility or blame be held against the publisher for reparation, damages, or monetary loss due to the information herein, either directly or indirectly.

Respective authors own all copyrights not held by the publisher.

The information herein is offered for informational purposes solely and is universal as such. The presentation of the information is without a contract or any guarantee assurance.

The trademarks used are without any consent, and the publication of the trademark is without permission or backing by the trademark owner. All trademarks and brands within this book are for clarifying purposes only and are owned by the owners themselves, not affiliated with this document.

You like to read, don't you?

Well, here's your chance to **get free ebooks** and **receive bonuses and gifts**!

Just click HERE or scan the follow QR code.

Table of Contents

Introduction 9

Chapter 1: What Is Microsoft Excel? 11

    1.1 What Is Excel Used For? 11

    1.2 History and Future of MS Excel 12

    1.3 Data Functions, Formulas, and Shortcuts 13

    1.4 Financial and Accounting Uses 13

Chapter 2: Why Learn Excel 2022? 14

    2.1 Why Use Formulas? 14

    2.2 How to Add Text to a Cell in Excel? 15

    2.3 Excel Multiplication Formula 15

    2.4 IF Function of Excel 16

    2.5 Excel Array Formula 17

    2.6 Average Formulas in Excel 17

    2.7 Percentage Formula in Excel 19

    2.8 Excel Variance Formula 19

Chapter 3: Basic Excel Formulas 22

    3.1 Five Time-Saving Ways to Insert Data into Excel 22

    3.2 Basic Formulas for Excel Workflow 25

    3.3 Excel Shortcuts 31

Chapter 4: Ten Advanced Excel Formulas 34

    4.1 Advanced Formulas 34

    4.2 Excel Formulas: The Cheat Sheet 41

Chapter 5: Modifying the Worksheet 44

    5.1 Moving to a Specific Cell 45

5.2 Adding a Row 45

5.3 Adding the Column 46

5.4 Shortcut Menu 46

5.5 Resizing a Column 46

5.6 Resizing a Row 47

5.7 Selecting a Cell 47

5.8 Cutting, Copying, and Pasting Cells 47

5.9 Keeping Headings Visible 48

Chapter 6: Five Ways Excel Can Improve Productivity During Your Work From Home 50

6.1 Processing Large Amounts of Data 50

6.2 Utilizing Fill Handles 50

6.3 Examining the Formulas All Simultaneously 50

6.4 Leverage the Goal Seek Formula 51

6.5 Automate Recurring Responsibilities With VBA 51

6.6 Best 49 Excel Templates to Increase or Boost Your Productivity 51

Chapter 7: Relative, Absolute, and Mixed Cell References in Excel 82

7.1 What Are Relative Cell References in Excel? 82

7.2 What are Absolute Cell References in Excel? 83

7.3 What Are Mixed Cell References in Excel? 85

7.4 How to Change the Reference From Relative to Absolute (or Mixed)? 86

7.5 Multiplication Table Using Mixed References 88

7.6 Multiplication Table Using an Array Formula 89

7.7 Create the Multiplication Table in Google Sheets 90

7.8 Numbering in Excel 90

Chapter 8: MS Excel: The WORKDAY.INTL Function 96

8.1 How to Use a WORKDAY.INTL Function in Excel? 98
8.2 WORKDAY.INTL Errors 99
8.3 MS Excel: The RANDBETWEEN Function 100
8.4 How to Use the RANDBETWEEN Function in Excel? ... 100
8.5 Tips for the RANDBETWEEN Function 101
8.6 Excel RAND Function 102

Chapter 9: MS Excel: The VLOOKUP Function 105
9.1 How to Use VLOOKUP in Excel? 106
9.2 VLOOKUP in Financial Modeling and Financial Analysis 108
9.3 Tips for the VLOOKUP Function 109
9.4 MS Excel: the HLOOKUP Function 111
9.5 How to Use the HLOOKUP Function in Excel? 111
9.6 Tips for HLOOKUP Function 114

Chapter 10: MS Excel: the TRANSPOSE Function (WS) 116
10.1 How to use the TRANSPOSE Function in Excel? 117
10.2 Tips for the TRANSPOSE Function 119
10.3 MS Excel: The COUNTBLANK Function 119
10.4 How to Use the COUNTBLANK Function in Excel? ... 120

Chapter 11: Convert Numbers into Words 122
11.1 How to Convert the Number into Words? 122

Chapter 12: Excel Data Entry Form 132
12.1 Parts of the Data Entry Form 134
12.2 Creating Another New Entry 135
12.3 Adding Data Entry Form Option 136
12.4 Navigating Through the Existing Records 138
12.5 Deleting a Record 140
12.6 How to Make a Data Entry Form in Excel? 141

12.7 How to Use the Data Validation Along With the Data Entry Form? 145

12.8 Formulas in Data Entry Forms 147

12.9 How to Open the Data Entry Form With VBA? 148

Chapter 13: Excel Valuation Modeling 151

13.1 Why Perform Valuation Modeling in Excel? 151

13.2 How to Execute Excel Valuation Modeling? 152

13.3 Jobs That Perform Valuation Modeling in Excel 154

13.4 Main Valuation Methods 155

Chapter 14: Mathematical and Statistical Functions 158

14.1 Excel Math Functions 158

14.2 Statistical Functions in Excel 160

Chapter 15: Use of Five Advanced Excel Pivot Table Techniques .. 163

15.1 Slicers 163

15.2 Timelines 164

15.3 Tabular View 166

15.4 Calculated Fields 167

15.5 Recommended Pivot Tables 169

Chapter 16: Create Charts in Excel: Types and Examples 171

16.1 Types of Charts 171

16.2 Step by Step Example of Creating Charts in Excel 172

16.3 Top Five Excel Chart and Graph Best Practices 191

16.4 How to Enter Chart Data in Excel? 192

Chapter 17: Excel Table 194

17.1 How to Create a Table in Excel? 195

17.2 How to Make a Table With a Selected Style? 196

17.3 How to Name a Table in Excel? 197

17.4 How to Use Tables in Excel? 197
17.5 How to Sort a Table in Excel? 198
17.6 How to Extend a Table in Excel? 200
17.7 How to Change Table Style? 201
17.8 How to Remove the Table Formatting? 201
17.9 How to Remove a Table in Excel? 202

Chapter 18: How to Become a Data Analyst in 2022? 203
18.1 What Does a Data Analyst Do? 203
18.2 What Is Data Analytics? 204
18.3 Data Analyst Qualifications 204
18.4 Data Analyst Responsibilities 205
18.5 What Tools Do Data Analysts Use? 207
18.6 Data Analysts Job 208
18.7 Data Analyst Salary 208
18.8 Data Analyst Career Path 209
18.9 Is Data Analysis a Growing Field? 210
18.10 How to Become a Data Analyst With No Experience? 211

Chapter 19: What Skills Should You Look for While Hiring an Excel Expert? 213
19.1 For Entry Level/Administrative Jobs 213
19.2 For Senior Level/Excel Specialists/Excel Experts 214
19.3 Business Analyst Excel Skills 214
19.4 Data Analyst Excel Skills 215
19.5 Auditor Excel Skills 216
19.6 Seven Tips to Improve Basic MS Excel Skills 216

Conclusion 219

YOUR GIFT 220

Thanks 221

Introduction

The book is built on a relatively straightforward idea. To understand, you must put in as much preparation time as possible. Not only can this assist you in being a more robust user of Microsoft Excel, but it will also provide you the courage to begin utilizing the app on your own, allowing you to build much more advanced applications capable of performing various tasks.

Furthermore, this book will assist you in learning a new ability, namely a complete comprehension of Microsoft Excel, but you will also benefit from extensive practice. So, essentially you will be studying and practicing various ideas, functions, and formulas you will have created your project or tiny app that you will use later throughout your personal, professional, or school life.

When it comes to Excel, there isn't much space for compromise. You have many beautiful clients because you're going to sing the songs on the spreadsheet every day. On the other side, many oppose it. They believe it is a row-and-column spreadsheet program, but specialized Excel theories focus on a diverse range of fundamental skills applicable and understood in almost every position within an organization. Since you've learned these concepts, you'll be better equipped to:

Since you've learned these concepts, you'll be better equipped to:

- Create algorithms that provide you more information about essential business functions, including workflow, project efficiency, financial predictions, and budget projections. It aids in inventory and consumption management.
- Provide an easy-to-use data collection tool for senior management to assess current activities or situations in an organization.

- Create spreadsheets that aid in the coordination of details to provide a clearer view of the latest data.
- Analyze and comprehend data from other governments, vendors, and customers.
- Allows consumers to access data in a more sophisticated way, including answers and solutions to industry problems.
- Maintain a healthy combination of financial and product data.
- Create reporting systems for a variety of agencies and programs using multiple automation procedures.

Advanced Excel training will provide businesses with highly skilled employees. Employees would perform more effectively in their current roles and move to higher-level positions because of it.

Many important features are included in the latest MS Excel features, allowing you to fully enjoy the potential of Excel.

- Increasing production and efficiency.
- To make yourself an integral part of the business.
- To make you great at data organizing and analyzing.
- To make the work go faster.
- To boost your results and production.

To summarize, It's always claimed that intelligence is power, and there's no better way to empower yourself than through sharpening your skills and the value of your company by knowledge and technology.

Chapter 1: What Is Microsoft Excel?

For data processing and analysis, Microsoft Excel is a valuable and efficient application. It's a database application of several columns and rows, with each intersection of a column and a row being referred to as a "cell." Each cell contains a single piece of data or information. You will render details easy to locate and instantly draw information from evolving data by grouping the data in this format.

Excel is a spreadsheet-based software application developed by Microsoft that uses formulas and functions to coordinate numbers and documents. Companies of all types utilize Excel analysis all around the world to do financial analysis.

1.1 What Is Excel Used For?

Excel is commonly used for data organization and financial reporting. It is seen in both corporate functions and for businesses of all sizes.

The following are some of Excel's most popular applications:

- Accounting
- Data entry
- Financial reporting
- Data maintenance
- Charting and graphing
- Programming
- Time management
- Task management
- Financial modeling
- Customer relationship management (CRM)

1.2 History and Future of MS Excel

Microsoft Excel played a critical part in bookkeeping and record-keeping for corporate activities in the early days of open PC business computing. A table with an auto sum format is one of the better instances of an MS Excel use case.

Entering a column of values and clicking into a cell at the bottom of the spreadsheet, then clicking the "auto sum" button to enable the cell to add up all the numbers entered above is quite simple in Microsoft Excel. This replaces manual ledger counts, which were a time-consuming aspect of the business before creating the modern spreadsheet.

MS Excel has been a must-have for different types of corporate computing, including looking at regular, weekly, or monthly figures, tabulating payroll and taxation, and other related business procedures, thanks to the auto sum and other advancements.

Thanks to various primary use cases, Microsoft Excel has been a critical end-user technology, effective in training and career growth. MS Excel has been included in simple business diploma courses on business computing for several years, and temporary job agencies can test individuals for various clerical duties based on their skills with Microsoft Word and Microsoft Excel.

On the other hand, Microsoft Excel has become increasingly outdated in several respects as enterprise technology has progressed. This is due to a term known as "visual dashboard" technology, also known as "data visualization."

In general, businesses and providers have devised innovative new approaches to visually display data that do not need end consumers to examine a conventional spreadsheet of columns of numbers and identifiers. Instead, they use diagrams, charts, and other sophisticated displays to help explain and comprehend the statistics. People also discovered that graphic presentations are much simpler to "read," and the concept of data visualization has changed Microsoft Excel's usage cases. Whereas in the past, companies may have used Microsoft Excel to manage hundreds of documents, today's company usage cases often include spreadsheets that handle just a few dozen values for each project.

If the spreadsheet has more than a few hundred rows, the details would be more successfully displayed on a visual dashboard than on a conventional spreadsheet format.

1.3 Data Functions, Formulas, and Shortcuts

Many features, algorithms, and shortcuts are included in the Excel software package that can be used to improve its functionality.

1.4 Financial and Accounting Uses

Excel is widely employed in the banking and accounting fields. Many businesses depend solely on Excel spreadsheets for their budgeting, planning, and accounting needs. Although Excel is an "information" processing method, the most popular data that is handled is financial data.

Excel is the ultimate financial software, according to Corporate Finance Institute (CFI). Although several pieces of financial software are designed to execute complex functions, Excel's robustness and openness are its best features. Excel templates should be as efficient as the analyst wants. Excel is used for accountants, investment managers, analysts, and individuals in all aspects of financial careers to fulfill their everyday tasks.

Chapter 2: Why Learn Excel 2022?

Excel is a widely used spreadsheet program. Despite the increase in prominence of rival programs like Google Sheets, Excel remains the most used method for data analysis in the world. Microsoft has refined and developed the app to render it as accessible and user-friendly as possible over the years. It's also convenient, allowing you to save time on a variety of activities.

Excel is not only a valuable application in daily life, but it is still a tool that is also widely employed in industries. Employers often mention the software as a prerequisite on career applications and having a good working experience will help you stick out. That's one of the basics when it comes to digital abilities. Data analytics is one field where there is a lot of demand.

2.1 Why Use Formulas?

The ability to utilize functions and formulas is one of Excel's most important capabilities. There is one distinction between these two terms:

- These are formulas. Some expressions can be used to measure cell values. Consider the following example: you may combine cells by writing out the formula =A1+A2+A3.

- Functions. There are Excel calculations that have been pre-programmed. They frequently result in a faster and more convenient way of completing activities in the software. As seen in the illustration below, the SUM function conducts the same calculation as the formula above. =SUM(A1:A3).

2.2 How to Add Text to a Cell in Excel?

There are a couple of choices accessible if you have a list of data and wish to add text to it. One thing you shouldn't do is type the terms in yourself. It can take a long time, and you'd be better off spending your time elsewhere. These Excel formulas are essential for those who work in the digital content creation industry since they can assist with handling product details.

Here are two forms to choose from:

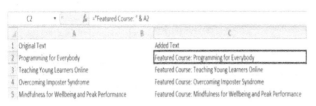

1. **"&" formula**: You may use this to add text before or after meaning in another cell. You include the cell you want to use and the text you want to use in speech marks. When you drag cell C2 away, the formula is automatically filled with the next cell in the sequence. ="Your Text " & A2 is the formula. As required, change the text and the cell number.

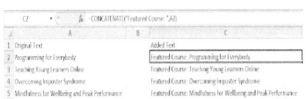

2. **Concatenate** is a valuable function. This mechanism is identical to the previous one, and it's beneficial for looping mutually many different cells. This feature allows you to merge a combination of text and data. =CONCATENATE ("Your Text," A2) is the function.

2.3 Excel Multiplication Formula

Excel may be used to perform multiplications in a variety of ways. The approach you choose is mainly determined by the kind of data you're dealing with and how you expect the product to appear. It's one of the key Excel formulas for personal and company accounting, such as bookkeeping.

These approaches include both basic and sophisticated techniques:

1. The * formula: The best way to multiply two values is to use the abbreviation (*) mark. To multiply seven by 5, for example, you'd write =7*5. While this is straightforward when dealing with two numbers, there are a few points to keep in mind when dealing with more complicated multiplications. If you enter =7*5+8*8, Excel can multiply 7 times 5, then add eight times 8, giving you 99. However, because Excel adds the 5 and 8 first (13) and then does seven times 13 times 8, =7*(5+8)*8 will result in 728.

2. The role of the PRODUCT: The PRODUCT feature makes it simple to calculate several numbers, cells, or cell ranges. It prevents you from having to type out an extended algorithm, which is particularly useful when dealing with many details. Consider the following scenario. It involves multiplication of all the values in column A using this formula function =PRODUCT and i.e., (A1:A5), which is far simpler than putting values one by one like (6*4*8*7*3)

	A	B	C	D	E
1	1				
2	4				
3	8				
4	7				
5	3				
6	672				
7					

A6 fx =PRODUCT(A1:A5)

2.4 IF Function of Excel

Excel's IF feature is beneficial and can be found in a variety of cases. There are few easier approaches to decide which cells follow those conditions when handling data than by utilizing an IF statement. It enables you to determine whether a value is real or false, depending on your information. If you start typing an IF sentence in Excel, you'll get the following outline that you must follow: (logical test, [value if true], [value if false]) =IF (logical test, [value if true], [value if false])

Let's say we want to grant a test a pass or fail rating depending on the results, with a passing mark of 60 or higher. The logical test determines whether the result is equivalent to or greater than 60. If the value is actual, the parameters are fulfilled; if the value if false is true, the criteria are not met. So, in Excel, we can write this as =IF(A1>=60,"

Pass," "Fail"). If the score in cell A1 is 60 or higher, then write "Pass." Whether It's less than 60, mark it as a failure.

2.5 Excel Array Formula

So far, we've focused on running a single procedure on a single collection of principles. But what if we need to apply a formula to several different items? Array formulas come in handy in this situation. You may use them to run operations on different values.

Array formula in Excel examines a set of individual values and conducts several calculations on one or more of them. It comes in handy for tasks like financial management.

Consider the following scenario. Let's assume you try to figure out the net amount of different products' purchases. Using an array formula instead of measuring subtotals for each class of the object and putting them together will save time and effort.

Then you type a function =SUM and (B2:B5*C2:C5) where you want the number to appear. The array formula is then completed using keyboard combination shortcuts such as Ctrl + Shift + Enter, also add the curly brackets in the formula. This function multiplies the standard values in the given list before adding the subtotals.

2.6 Average Formulas in Excel

Let's go back to high school math for a moment (sorry!). The mean, median, and mode are the three major forms of averages, as you can recall. Excel is a useful method for data processing, and it will help you search for each of these averages. If you need a fast pick-me-up, try these:

17

1. Mean. Add all the percentages together and split them by the number of numbers you have.

2. The median. When the numbers are in size order, the amount in the center.

3. Mode. In a series of numbers, the number that appears the most.

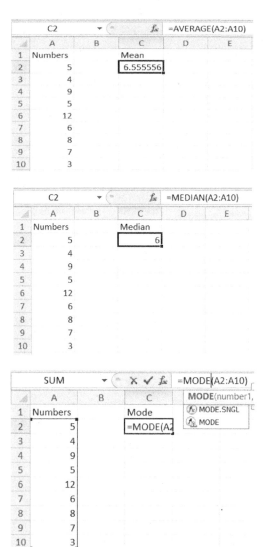

2.7 Percentage Formula in Excel

There are some Excel formulas as helpful as percentage calculations when it comes to critical Excel formulas. There are some basic ways to measure or display percentages:

- Make a fraction out of a decimal. If your values are being shown decimals rather than percentages, simply press the percent icon on the top bar to convert them to percentages.
- As a percentage of the total, to measure the percentage (A1) of the total (B1), type = A1/B1 in the cell where you want to calculate the percentage. And press the percent button to see the result as a percentage.
- A percentage increases. This time, a basic calculation will help you out. In one cell, write your starting value, and in another, write the percentage you want to raise. The formula =A1*(1+B1) is used in the illustration below. Shift the + to a - with a percentage drop.

	A	B	C	D	E
1	100	35%	135		
2					
3					

(C1, f_x =A1*(1+B1))

2.8 Excel Variance Formula

Variance is a measure of how dispersed a set of data is. A significant variance, for example, indicates that the data points are widely apart from the mean average and each other. It may be used in investing in measuring how assets in a portfolio work against each other and the average. Excel has several functions for calculating variance. Both determine whether you want to calculate the variation in a survey or the whole population and whether you want to measure or disregard text and logical principles.

We'll concentrate on the regular variance feature to keep it simple. This lacks text and abstract values in favor of data samples. The VAR.S feature is shown in the following example:

	D2		fx	=VAR.S(B2:B8)

	A	B	C	D
1	Student	Score		Variance
2	Student 1	85		63.95238095
3	Student 2	74		
4	Student 3	72		
5	Student 4	90		
6	Student 5	88		
7	Student 6	76		
8	Student 7	71		

You may also use the formula =STDEV.S to calculate the standard deviation of this same package (B2:B8).

2.8.1 Excel Profit Chart

So far, we've just covered the most basic Excel formulas and functions. We're going to take this a bit further with our final point. Excel is useful for spreadsheets and data organization, but It's still great for viewing data once you've analyzed it. Let's look at creating a basic Excel profit chart that shows how much profit a company generated during a specific period. Here is how the table appears:

	D12		fx		
	A	B	C	D	E
1	Month	Income	Expenses	Profit	
2	January	2,350	565	1,785	
3	February	2,400	380	2,020	
4	March	2,580	700	1,880	
5	April	2,700	654	2,046	
6	May	3,000	950	2,050	
7	June	2,860	650	2,210	
8					
9			Total	11,991	

While the data is shown, it is not the most visually pleasing way to do so. Instead, you can transform that into a graph that shows a different perspective on the profit. It's a straightforward procedure that can be done with a single mouse press.

To begin, go to the top of Excel and select the "Insert" key. Following that, you'll see a variety of chart and graph choices. When you choose one of these options, the data from your spreadsheet will automatically populate the display:

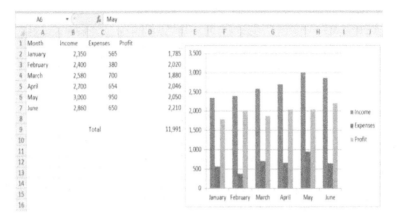

You may format the chart here by changing the design, colors, details, and various other features. Excel is still a reasonable option because you need to view the data straightforwardly and concisely. That concludes our list of Excel's most valuable tips and tricks. If you can see, you cannot only do a lot for the app, but you can still do it in many different contexts. When it comes to data analysis, a little knowledge will save you time and effort.

Chapter 3: Basic Excel Formulas

For initiators to become extremely skilled in financial research, they must first master the simple Excel formulas. Microsoft Excel is widely regarded as the industry norm of data processing applications. In terms of data analysis, financial modeling, and presentation, Microsoft's spreadsheet program is one of the most common among investment bankers and financial analysts. There are two basic terms:

1. **Formulas:** A formula in Excel is an equation that works for values in several cells or a single cell. e.g., =A1+A2+A3 calculates the number of the values in cells A1 through A3.
2. **Functions:** In MS Excel, we call the functions predefined formulas. They do away with the time-consuming manual entry we normally follow when using these formulas by simply assigning them easy to remember titles. =SUM, for example (A1:A3). The function adds up all the values in the range A1 to A3.

3.1 Five Time-Saving Ways to Insert Data into Excel

There are five popular ways to incorporate simple Excel formulas while analyzing results. Each plan has its own set of benefits. As a result, before we get through the essential

formulas, let's go through specific strategies so you can set up your favorite workflow right away.

1. **Simple insertion:** Inserting standard Excel formulas is as simple as typing a formula in a cell or using the formula bar. Typically, the procedure begins with an equal sign accompanied by the name of an Excel feature.
Excel is clever in that it displays a pop-up function clue as you start typing the function word. You'll choose your choice from this page. Do not, however, click the Enter key. Instead, click the Tab key to begin inserting additional choices. Otherwise, you could get an invalid name mistake, which looks like

"#NAME?" Simply pick the cell again and complete the role in the formula bar.

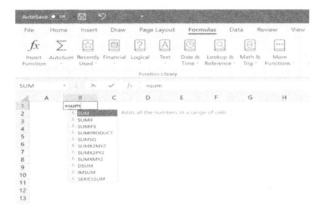

2. **Using the insert function option from the formulas tab:** The Excel Insert Feature dialogue box is what you need if you want complete power of your function insertion. To do so, go to the Formulas tab and pick Insert Function from the first menu. Many of the roles you'll need to finish the financial report will be available in the dialogue box.

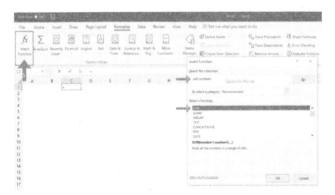

3. **Selecting the desired formulas from "Formula Tab":** This tab provides quick access to your or desired formulas, to access this tab simply click on the "formula" tab given in the top ribbon then find out your desired formula in the respective category. Most of the formulas are already given under this tab but just in case you are unable to find out your desired

formula then you can click on "more functions" this option will open up some more stuff for you.

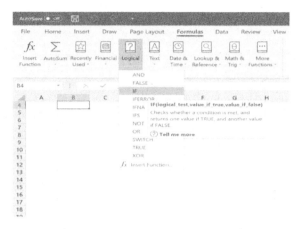

4. **Using "AutoSum" option:** The AutoSum feature is your go-to option for daily and straightforward tasks. So, go to the Home tab and press the AutoSum option in the far-right corner. Then press the caret to reveal other formulas that were previously covered. This alternative is also available after the Insert Function option on the Formulas page.

5. **Quick insert:** Using the Recently Used menu instead of retyping the most recent formula if you find it repetitive. It's present on the Formulas page, right next to AutoSum, as the third menu selection.

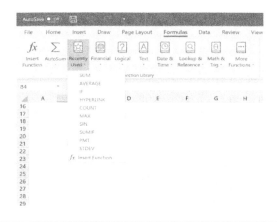

3.2 Basic Formulas for Excel Workflow

3.2.1 SUM

The SUM feature is the first Excel formula that you can learn. Values from a selection of columns or rows from the chosen settings are normally aggregated.

=SUM (number1, [number2], …)

For example:

"=SUM(A10:A12)" This formula will add up all the values given in the range starting from Cell A10 and ending at A12.

"=SUM(B2:G2)" This formula will add up all the values given in the range starting from Cell B2 and ending at G8.

"=SUM(B2:B7,B9,B12:B15)" Now this formula is a little bit advance as it will start to function in such a way that it will add up all the values given in the range from B2 to B7 then it will omit any value in cell B8, then it will add up the value given in B9, now again it will omit all the value in cell B10 to B11 and add up all the values of B12 to B15.

"=SUM(A2:A8)" using this given formula and dividing It by 20 will give you a result in which you can turn your fraction into a simple formula.

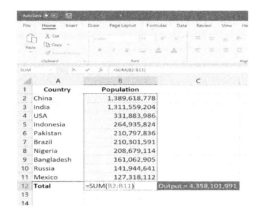

3.2.2 Use of AVERAGE

This function helps to find out the simple averages for a given set of data i.e. you can easily calculate the average results, of the stockholder in a shareholding pool to do that you can use the given formula

"=AVERAGE" followed by this syntax which includes (number 1,2,3 and so on …)"

For example:

"=AVERAGE(B4:B12)" this formula will result in an average value of a range starting from B4 and ending at B12.

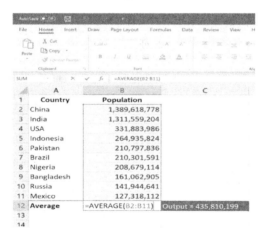

26

3.2.3 COUNT

The COUNT feature counts the number of cells in a set that only includes numeric values.

For example, the formula given here =COUNT and insert (value1,[value2]...) will count the numeric values.

For example:

COUNT (A:A) this function will help you to count all the given values in a set that are numerical and are lying at A. You are required to modify the range for counting the rows.

e.g., COUNT and insert (A1:C1) – Now, it can count rows.

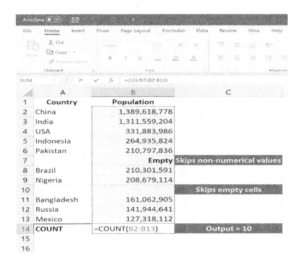

3.2.4 COUNTA

COUNTA, like the COUNT feature, counts all cells in a rage. It does, however, count all cells, regardless of their kind. Unlike COUNT, which only counts numerically, this function often counts days, hours, sequences, logical values, mistakes, null strings, and text.

=COUNTA (value1, [value2], ...)

For example:

"COUNTA(C2:C13)" this given formula can count the number of rows starting from 2 to 13 inside column C, No matter what is the type of your data. However, like in the case of the COUNT function, a user can't use the same or exact formula for counting the number of rows. While using this formula a user must adjust the range inside the brackets—for example, the formula "COUNTA(C2:H2)" will result in a total count of values gin in column C to H.

3.2.5 IF

When you choose to sort the data according to a set of rules, the IF feature is often used. The nice thing about the IF formula is that it allows you to use formulas and functions.

For example, the syntax =IF followed by any logical test, then true or false if the value is true the result will be true otherwise false.

For example:

=IF (J2<K3, "TRUE" else "FALSE")—this function will test if any value given in the cell K3 is greater than the cell value at

J2. The results will be true or false depending upon the logic of the function.

An example to understand this complicated IF logic can be: "=IF(B2>C2,True,False)" Now this function will check if any value given in the cell B2 is greater than the cell value of C2 then it will show "True" in the column where the formula is being typed otherwise it will result in "False" value in the cell.

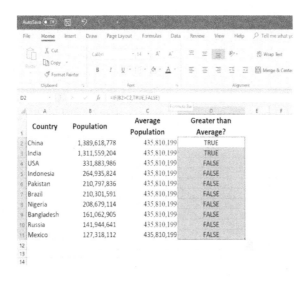

3.2.6 TRIM

The TRIM function ensures that unruly spaces do not cause errors in your functions. It means that there are no vacant spaces. TRIM only works on a single cell, unlike other functions that may work on a group of cells. As a result, it has the drawback of duplicating details in a spreadsheet.

Function like =TRIM (text)

For example:

e.g., TRIM(A2): Eliminates the empty places in the cell A2 value.

3.2.7 MAX & MIN

The functions Max and MIN are normally used to find out the greatest and smallest values in a given set. The function will be as follows.

First of all type "=" sign then enter "MIN or Max" then select the number or a range.

For example:

=MIN(C15:C20) this formula will result in a minimum value residing in the range of C15 to C20 similarly you can replace the "MIN" with "MAX" to find out the maximum value.

For example:

Type =MAX and select a range starting from B2 and ending at C11— Similarly, it will find a maximum number in this given range.

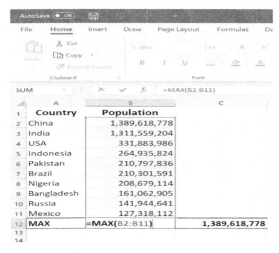

3.3 Excel Shortcuts

Before digging into Excel shortcuts, It's a good idea to go through the standard vocabulary for the various Excel components.

- Any of the several boxes in the Excel spreadsheet is referred to as a cell.
- An active cell is the one that Excel is selecting. There can only be one functioning cell at any given time.

- The active cell, or a community of cells, is referred to as a selection. If the range contains more than one cell, the active cell will be outlined in white, while the remainder of the selection will be grey.
- A column is a collection of vertical cells in Excel referred to by letters ranging from A to Z. Excel can repeat letters a second time after column Z. As a result, and column AA is the next column after column Z, preceded by column AB.
- A row is a set of horizontal cells in Excel referred to by integers in ascending order from 1 to n. The value of n varies depending on the operating system and Excel version.
- Inside Excel, there are many various types of data.
- Text is a type of data that is made up of letters. Text data may also contain numbers. On the other hand, these amounts must be used in combination with letters or manually set to text.
- Numbers are records that are solely made up of numbers. Digit type data cannot use characters, unlike text type data, which does.
- Numbers are used in combination with a currency marker in currency/accounting info.
- Dates are bits of information that represent a date and/or period. In Excel, dates may be formatted in a variety of ways.
- Data of the percentage kind is a form of numbered data that has been translated to a percentage. These can be translated back into data of the number kind, and vice versa. When you convert a percentage to an integer, the result is a decimal. 89 percent, for example, would be converted to 0.89.

3.3.1 Why Use Excel Shortcuts?

Using Excel shortcuts or shortcut keys is an often-overlooked way of efficiency while operating with an Excel model. When used instead of clicking in the toolbar, these shortcut keys execute extensive functions that significantly improve performance and speed. Consider hitting just two to three keys on the keyboard rather than shifting the hand to the cursor, moving the button, then clicking several times.

There are hundreds or thousands of shortcuts available for excel that can be used to make your work easy and hassle-free. The usage of these shortcuts may vary from finding out a specific formula to navigation among spreadsheets.

3.3.2 Excel Shortcuts Example

	A	B	C	D
1		Price	Quantity	Total Price
2	Orange	$ 1.00	5	$ 5.00
3	Tomato	$ 2.00	10	$ 20.00
4	Potato	$ 3.00	20	$ 60.00

These pieces of data only show columns A to D and rows 1 to 4.

The given snapshot contains a selection from A2–D2 hence this given range would be referenced inside the MS Excel formula bar as (A2:D2).

There can always be one active cell, no matter how much selection a user has made the active cell will always have an orange color.

Cells from A2 to A4 include the text data [Orange, Tomato, and the Potato]

Cells from B1 to D2 include the text data [Quantity, Price, and the Total Price]

Cells from B2 to B4 and D2 to D4 include currency data, denoted in the dollar sign "$"

Cells from C2 to C4 include number data.

Chapter 4: Ten Advanced Excel Formulas

Any financial analyst invests much more time in Excel than he or she would like to say. We've gathered the most relevant and sophisticated Excel formulas that any world-class financial analyst should recognize based on years of practice.

4.1 Advanced Formulas

4.1.1 Index Match

Formula is given as: =INDEX (C3 ratio E9, MATCH (B13, C3 ratio C9,0), MATCH (B14, C3 ratio E3,0))

INDEX MATCH is a versatile Excel formula mix that can help you improve your financial research and modeling. INDEX is a table function that returns the value of a cell depending on the column and row number.

MATCH returns the row or column direction of a cell.

Here's an example of combining the INDEX and MATCH formulas. We look up and return a person's height based on their name in this case. We should adjust both the name and the height in the calculation since they are both factors.

	A	B	C	D	E	F	G
1							
2			1	2	3		
3		1	Name	Height	Weight		
4		2	Sally	6.2	185		
5		3	Tom	5.9	170		
6		4	Kevin	5.8	175		
7		5	Amanda	5.5	145		
8		6	Carl	6.1	210		
9		7	Ned	6.0	180		
10							
11							
12			=INDEX(C3:E9,MATCH(B13,C3:C9,0),MATCH(B14,C3:E3,0))				
13		Kevin					
14		Height					

4.1.2 IF in Combination With AND/OR

The formula is given as:

=IF (AND (C2 is greater or equal to C4, C2 is less or equal to C5), C6, C7)

Anyone who has disbursed a significant amount of time working with different financial models understands how difficult nested IF formulas can be. Combining the IF feature with the AND / OR function will make formulas simpler to audit and appreciate for other users. You will see how we combined the individual functions to construct a more advanced formula in the illustration below.

	A	B	C	D	E	F	G
1							
2		Data Cell		150			
3							
4		Condition 1		100	>=		
5		Condition 2		999	<=		
6		Result if true		100			
7		Result if fales		0			
8							
9		Live Formula		=IF(AND(C2>=C4,C2<=C5),C6,C7)			
10							
11							

4.1.3 OFFSET in Combination With SUM or AVERAGE

The formula is given as:

=SUM (B4 ratio OFFSET (B4,0, E2 minus 1))

The OFFSET function isn't very complex on its own, but when combined with other functions like SUM or AVERAGE, we can construct a complicated formula. Consider the following scenario: you want to build a complex feature that can sum a variable number of cells. You can only do a static calculation using the average SUM formula, but you can shift the cell relation around by adding OFFSET.

If it operates is as follows: To make this formula work, we use the OFFSET function instead of the SUM function's ending comparison cell. This makes the formula complex, and you can say Excel how many sequential cells you want to sum up in the cell referenced as E2. We have those advanced Excel algorithms now. This much more a complex formula is shown in the screenshot below.

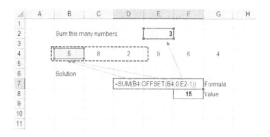

4.1.4 CHOOSE

The formula is given as:

=CHOOSE (Choice, option 1, 2, 3)

The CHOOSE role is ideal for financial simulation scenario study. It encourages you to choose from a set of choices and can return the "choice" you've made. Assume you have three separate sales growth projections for next year: 5%, 12%, and 18%. If you tell Excel, you want option #2, and you will get a 12 percent return using the CHOOSE formula.

	A	B	C	D	E	F	G
1							
2							
3			Option 1	5%			
4			Option 2	12%			
5			Option 3	18%			
6							
7		Selection ->	2	=CHOOSE(C7,D3,D4,D5)			
8							
9							
10							
11							

4.1.5 XNPV and XIRR

Formula: = XNPV (discount rate, cash flows, dates)

These calculations can prove useful if you work in investment management, market research, financial planning & analysis (FP&A), or some other field of corporate finance that includes discounting cash flows.

Simply placed, XNPV and XIRR enable you to assign separate dates to each discounted cash flow. The simple NPV and IRR formulas in Excel have the flaw in assuming that the time intervals between cash flows are equivalent. As an economist, you'll see conditions where cash balances aren't equally spaced regularly, and this formula is how you solve it.

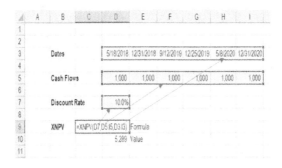

4.1.6 SUMIF and COUNTIF

Formula: = COUNTIF (D5 ratio D12," is greater or equal than 21")

Conditional functions are used effectively in these two developed formulas. All cells that need specific criteria are included in SUMIF, and all cells that need measures are counted in COUNTIF. For example, suppose you may want to figure out how many containers of champagne you need for a client event by counting all cells that are larger than or equivalent to 21 (the minimum consumption age in the United States). As seen in the screenshot given below, COUNTIF may be used as an advanced approach.

	A	B	C	D	E	F	G	H
1								
2								
3								
4				Age				
5				19				
6				26				
7				20				
8				19				
9				29				
10				31				
11				21				
12				25				
13								
14				=COUNTIF(D5:D12,">=21")				
15								

4.1.7 PMT and IPMT

Formula: =PMT (# of periods, interest rate, present value)

You'll need to know these two formulas if you operate in real estate, commercial banking, FP&A, or other financial analyst jobs that deal with debt schedules.

The PMT theorem calculates the worth of making equivalent payments throughout a loan's existence. You should do that in combination with IPMT (which shows you how much interest you'll pay for the same kind of loan), then different principal and interest payments. Here's how to use the PMT feature to calculate the annual mortgage payment on a $1 million loan with a 5% interest rate over 30 years.

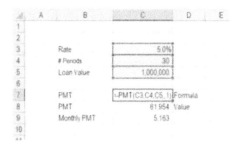

4.1.8 LEN and TRIM

Formulas are given below:

=TRIM (text) &

=LEN (text)

The formulas mentioned above are a little less general, but they are complex. Financial experts who need to manage and manipulate vast volumes of data may benefit from them. Unfortunately, the data we receive is not necessarily well-organized, and problems such as extra spaces at the beginning or end of cells will arise.

The LEN formula returns the number of characters in a specified text string, which is helpful when you need to count how many characters are in a text. You will see how the TRIM algorithm cleans up the Excel data in the illustration below.

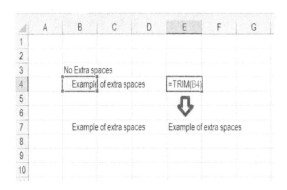

4.1.9 CONCATENATE

The formula is given as:

39

=A1&"more text."

Concatenate isn't even a function in and of itself; It's just a creative way of bringing data from multiple cells together and making worksheets more complex. For financial analysts doing financial simulation, this is a valuable instrument.

In the illustration below, the text "New York" plus "," is combined with "NY" to form "New York, NY." This enables you to make dynamic worksheet headers and labels. Instead of upgrading cell B8, you will also upgrade cells B2 and D2 independently. This is a great attribute to have while dealing with vast data collection.

	A	B	C	D	E	F
1						
2		New York		NY		
3						
4						
5		=B2&", "&D2				
6		⇩				
7						
8		New York, NY				
9						
10						
11						

4.1.10 CELL, MID, LEFT, and RIGHT Functions

These complex Excel features may be merged to produce specific, very complicated, and advanced formulas. The CELL feature may return a range of data about a cell's contents (such as its name, location, row, column, and more). The LEFT function returns the text from the cell's beginning (left to right), the MID function returns the text from any cell's start point (left to right), and the RIGHT function returns the text from the cell's end (right to the left).

The three formulations are shown in the diagram below.

	A	B	C	D	E	F
1						
2						
3		New York, NY		=LEFT(B3,3)	⇨	New
4						
5				=MID(B3,5,4)	⇨	York
6						
7				=RIGHT(B3,2)	⇨	NY
8						
9						
10						
11						

4.2 Excel Formulas: The Cheat Sheet

You've come to the right spot if you want to learn Excel financial analysis and become an expert at designing financial models. We've put together an Excel formula cheat sheet with the most vital formulas and functions you'll need to master spreadsheets.

4.2.1 Time and Date in Excel Formulas of Cheat Sheet

- =EDATE—add a specific quantity of month's date in Excel.
- =DATE—Yields a number representing the date (yyyy/mm/dd) in Excel.
- =EOMONTH—change a date to the month last day (e.g., from 7/18/2018 to 7/31/2018)
- =YEAR—extracts and displays the year from a date (e.g., 7/18/2018 to 2018) in Excel.
- =YEARFRAC—conveys the fraction of a year between two dates (e.g., 1/1/2018 – 3/31/2018 = 0.25)
- =NETWORKDAYS—Yields the number of entire workdays between the two specified dates.
- =TODAY—add and show today's date in a cell.
- Convert time to seconds—converts an amount of time to seconds (e.g., 5 minutes to 300 seconds)

4.2.2 Navigation Excel Formulas for Cheat Sheet

- Go to Special and click on F5 and find all the cells that are hard-codes, formulas, and more.
- Find and Replace—press Ctrl + F, and you can change parts of many formulas at once.

4.2.3 Lookup Formulas

- INDEX MATCH—a combination of lookup functions that are much effective than VLOOKUP.
- =VLOOKUP—the lookup functions that pursuits vertically in a table.
- =HLOOKUP—the lookup functions that pursuits horizontally in a table.
- =INDEX—a lookup function that pursuits vertically and horizontally in a table.
- =MATCH—returns the position of a value in a series.

- =OFFSET—moves the reference of a cell by the number of rows and/or columns specified.

4.2.4 Math Functions for Excel Formulas for Cheat Sheet

- =SUM—add the sum of a set of numbers.
- =AVERAGE—evaluates the average of a set of numbers.
- =MEDIAN—reverts the median average number of a set.
- =SUMPRODUCT—evaluates the weighted average, very helpful for financial analysis.
- =PRODUCT—multiplies all a series of numbers.
- =ROUNDDOWN—rounds a number to the specified number of digits.
- =ROUNDUP—the formula rounds a number to the specific number of digits.
- AutoSum—a shortcut to quickly figure a series of numbers.
- =ABS—reverts the absolute value of a number.
- =PI—reverts the value of π, precise to 15 digits.
- =SUMQ—reverts the sum of the squares of the arguments
- =SUMIF—the sum values in a scale that are restricted by a condition.

4.2.5 Financial Formulas

- =NPV—determines the remaining present value of cash flows centered on a discount rate.
- =XNPV—determines the NPV of cash flows based on specific dates and discount rate.
- =IRR—this formula calculates the internal rate of return (the discount rate that adjusts the NPV to zero.
- =XIRR—determines the internal rate of return (the discount rate that adjusts the NPV to zero) with specific dates.
- =YIELD—returns the yield of a guarantee based on face value, maturity, and interest rate.
- =FV—determines the upcoming value of investing with constant periodic payments and a constant interest rate.
- =PV—determines the present value of an investment.
- =INTRATE—the interest rate on an entirely invested security.
- =IPMT—this formula yields the interest payments (debt security).
- =PMT—this function yields the complete payment (debt as well as interest) on a debt security.

- =PRICE—calculates the price per $100 face value of a recurring coupon bond.
- =DB—determines the depreciation based on the stable-declining balance method.
- =DDB—determines the depreciation based on the dual-declining balance method.
- =SLN—determines the depreciation based on the successive-line method.

4.2.6 Conditional Functions

- =IF—checks if a condition is met and returns a value if yes and if no.
- =OR—it checks if any of the conditions are met and yields only "FALSE" or "TRUE."
- =XOR—the "exclusive or" assertion yields true if the number of TRUE statements is odd.
- =AND—checks if all conditions are met and returns only "TRUE" or "FALSE."
- =NOT—changes "TRUE" to "FALSE" and "FALSE" to "TRUE."
- IF AND—combine IF with AND to have numerous conditions.
- =IFERROR—if a cell consists of a mistake or error, you may tell Excel to show an alternate result.

4.2.7 Other Functions and Formulas

- Sheet Name Code—a formula using MID, CELL, and FIND functions to display the worksheet name.
- Consolidate—how to establish the piece of information among the multiple Excel workbooks.

Chapter 5: Modifying the Worksheet

Connect data to a cell; rotate across cells; add columns and rows to a spreadsheet; cut, duplicate, and paste cells; and resize columns, and rows are all covered in this segment. It also demonstrates how to use the freeze pane's function, which helps you freeze column and row headings to make navigating a big worksheet easier.

- **Adding information to a cell:** To enter data into a cell, press it with your mouse and start typing.
- **Moving about within cells:** Use the keyboard commands mentioned below to navigate through the worksheet cells.

Movement Action	Key Combination
One cell up	Up arrow key or +
One cell down	Down arrow key or key
One cell left	Left arrow key or +
One cell right	Right arrow key or key
Top of the worksheet (cell A1)	+
End of the worksheet (last cell containing data)	<Ctrl< +

End of the row	+ Right arrow key
End of the column	+ Down arrow key

5.1 Moving to a Specific Cell

For moving into a specific cell:

1. Enter the address of a cell in the Name Box.

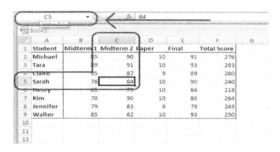

2. Press on the entering icon on your keyboard.
3. For moving cells, click on any given cell by using arrow keys. The cell become active when you move through the cell. Click on CTRL + an arrow key and start scrolling in a column or row. Use cut, copy, and paste keys for moving through the cells.
4. Choose the range of cells. Click CTRL + C and then CTRL + V.

5.2 Adding a Row

A row is a horizontal line that extends through a worksheet. To connect a row to a worksheet, do the following:

1. Choose the worksheet on which you want the row to appear.
2. Choose the Home tab from the drop-down menu.
3. In the Cells group, click the arrow on the Insert button.
4. Select Insert Sheet Rows from the drop-down menu.

5.3 Adding the Column

A column goes vertically down a worksheet. For adding a column, follow the steps:

1. Choose the worksheet on which you want the column to appear.
2. Choose the Home tab from the drop-down menu.
3. In the Cells group, click the arrow on the Insert button.
4. Select Insert Sheet Columns from the drop-down menu.

5.4 Shortcut Menu

For inserting rows or columns, use the shortcut menu.

1. To add a new row or column, press the column letter or row number where you want it to appear.
2. If you're using a PC, right-click on the row number/column letter; if you're using a Mac, control-click the row number/column label. A menu with shortcuts would appear.
3. From the shortcut menu, choose Insert.

5.5 Resizing a Column

For resizing a column, follow the steps:

1. Select the worksheet by clicking somewhere on it.
2. Move the cursor along the column heading's border before it switches to a plus symbol.
3. Click and drag the column width before you're comfortable about it.

5.6 Resizing a Row

For resizing a row, follow the steps:

1. Select the worksheet by clicking somewhere on it.
2. Move the cursor along the row heading's border before it switches to a plus symbol.
3. Drag the width of the row before you're comfortable about it.

5.7 Selecting a Cell

You must first choose a cell before you can change or format it. The table below shows you how to pick cells quickly.

Cells to Select	Mouse Action
One cell	Click once in the cell
Entire row	Click the row heading
Entire column	Click the column heading
Entire worksheet	Click the **Select All** button located above the row headings and to the left of the column headings, or press **Ctrl + A** on your keyboard.
Cluster of cells	Click and drag the mouse over the cell cluster

5.8 Cutting, Copying, and Pasting Cells

To switch cells from one spot on a worksheet to another, first copy or cut the cell(s), then paste the cell or cells in their current location.

To cut a cell, do the following:

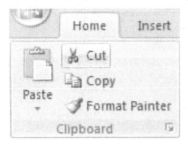

1. To select a cell, click it.
2. Choose the Home tab from the drop-down menu.
3. Press Ctrl + X on your screen or click on the Cut button in the Clipboard cluster.

To copy a cell, do the following:

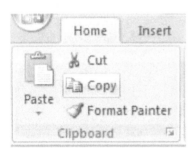

1. To choose a cell, click it.
2. Choose the Home tab from the drop-down menu.
3. Press Ctrl + C on your screen or click the Copy button in the Clipboard cluster.

To paste a cut or copied cell to a new location on your worksheet, do the following:

1. To find a new location on your worksheet, click it.
2. Choose the Home tab from the drop-down menu.
3. Press Ctrl + V on the keyboard or click the Paste button in the Clipboard group.

5.9 Keeping Headings Visible

If you have a big worksheet with many columns and row headings, they can fade when you scroll down. You should use the Freeze Panes option if you want the headings to always stay clear. Separately freezing the column and row headings is needed.

To keep the row headings frozen, do the following:

1. On the left side of the worksheet, click the Row 1 heading.
2. Choose View from the drop-down menu.
3. In the Window group, click the Freeze Panes icon.

4. Choose Freeze Top Row from the menu.
5. To freeze the column headings, do the following:
6. At the top of the worksheet, click the Column A heading.
7. Choose View from the drop-down menu.
8. In the Window group, click the Freeze Panes icon.
9. Choose Freeze First Column from the drop-down menu.

Chapter 6: Five Ways Excel Can Improve Productivity During Your Work From Home

6.1 Processing Large Amounts of Data

There's a fair chance you're dealing around vast volumes of numbers, whether you're a data scientist or an account manager. These days, big data is everywhere, and Excel is one of the most robust methods for working with it. Excel allows data analysis simple with features including pivot tables. A pivot table allows you to quickly organize and sort raw data into easy-to-understand tables by rearranging the columns. You will save time and gain strategic insights more quickly this way.

6.2 Utilizing Fill Handles

Most people copy the formula from the 1st row of the table to the last row while applying formulas to tables. You can paste a whole column of calculations with only a few keystrokes if you understand the data-navigating keyboard cutoffs in Excel. Fill handles, on the other side, are much faster, so you don't have to go to the bottom of the table. The fill handle is the rectangle in the lower right corner of an Excel selection. Simply double-click the fill handle in a column next to another column with a complete collection of data to copy the formula to the bottom of the table. This allows you to produce far more extensive spreadsheets with far less time.

6.3 Examining the Formulas All Simultaneously

Excel displays the formula instead of the outcome if you edit a cell that holds a formula. The keyboard shortcut "Control +" can be used to see all the calculations on a worksheet at once. You can alter as many formulas as you like nearly instantly when you use this shortcut. It's a smart way to guarantee the consistency and fluidity of the sheet.

6.4 Leverage the Goal Seek Formula

Goal Seek is an Excel feature that shows you how one data element in a formula affects another. Since you can easily change a single cell entry to see the outcome, It's a handy method for answering "what if" questions. It's particularly useful in economics, revenue, and predicting scenarios because it allows you to see how predictions could shift if one variable is changed. Use it, choose "What If Analysis" and "Goal Seek" from the drop-down menus in a cell.

6.5 Automate Recurring Responsibilities With VBA

One of Excel's most useful methods is Virtual Basic of Applications (VBA). If you're used to hours of manual data entry, VBA will reduce it to only a few minutes with this simple macro. When operating at home or the hospital, this can be a big-time saver and help. Microsoft Excel is a time-saving program that will help you get a lot more done at work.

6.6 Best 49 Excel Templates to Increase or Boost Your Productivity

Using Microsoft Excel models saves you not only time but also boosts your efficiency. Act without thinking about your workbook's architecture and stop having to create complicated formulas from scratch by using models.

There's a blueprint for anything in Excel: basic spreadsheets, product control, budgets, analytics, and surveys, and task management. Fortunately, you won't have to search for hours to locate the right one. We've always finished the legwork for you.

Our experienced team has put together a compilation of the best 51 Excel models to help you improve your job and efficiency.

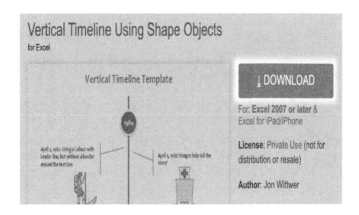

1. **Family Budget Planner**

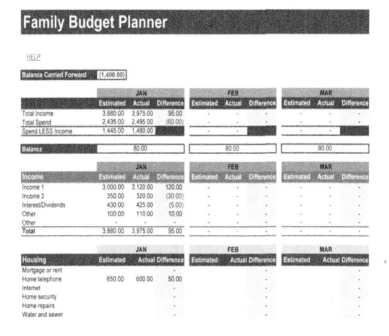

With this essential but incredibly useful guide, you can keep track of finances within your family or team. You will easily optimize the investments with fields for overall revenue, personal profits, spending, and other fields.

2. Personal Budget Spreadsheet

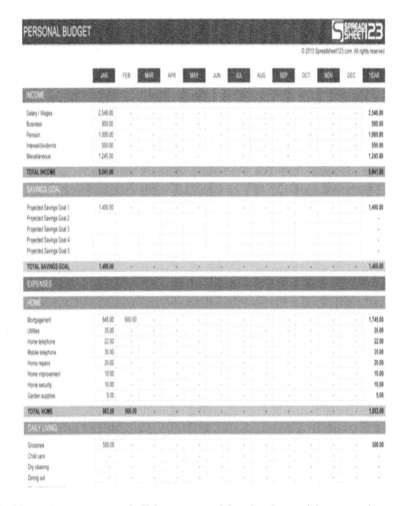

Working on your own? This personal budget enables you to get a clearer, more detailed picture of your revenue, expenses, and potential savings.

3. Household Budget Planner

This budgeting guide provides maps and a summary of monthly costs that you can tailor to meet the needs of your staff. If you're curious about how to make a household budget in Excel, this template can give you the answer.

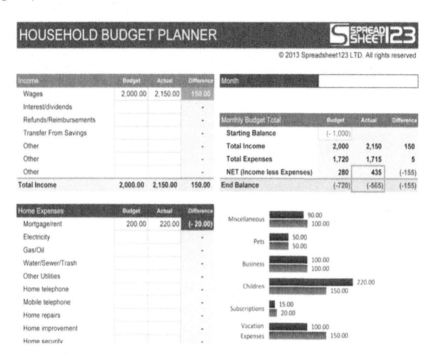

4. Weekly Budget Worksheet

You don't want to overthink ahead of time? Concentrate on the present moment and use a monthly budget planner. You'll also be able to note important information on how you manage your money when you fill up the planner.

Event Fundraiser

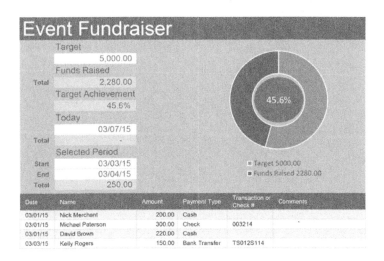

If you're collecting money for a case, It's essential to keep track of who supported, how much they gave, and the

overall amount required. This template changes automatically when you enter data and displays a graphic chart to get a short overview.

5. **Social Media Calendar**

Are you a social networking genius? Use this premium template to schedule your upcoming posts down to the minute they go live.

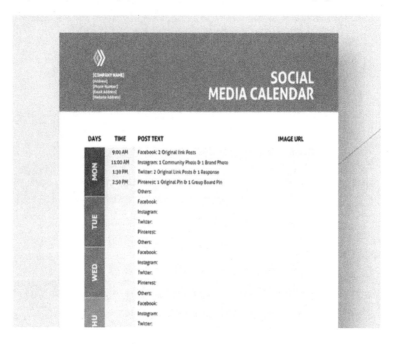

6. Project Gantt Chart

This advanced and versatile template allows you to handle plans, money, and deliverables with precision. Using this Gannt chart design, you will keep track of all your project's deliverables.

7. Net Worth Statement

![Net Worth Statement form]

If you know how much money you're worth right now? If you don't know how to measure it, use this essential yet powerful guide. "It's your consumption patterns, not your income, that render you wealthy."

8. Bubble Chart Timeline

Using the smaller bubbles, add different divisions and detail while using the main timeline to provide a broad summary.

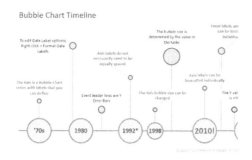

9. Employee Payroll Register

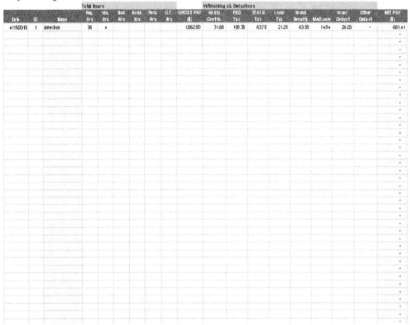

Employers can help handle payrolls using this template. To correctly measure their salaries, keep track of employee records, payroll expenses, and hours employed.

10. Employee Scheduling Template

Browse the calendar templates and choose the Excel calendar template which best suits your needs. On the template page, click the Download option, open template file in Excel, or thereafter modify and save your calendar. Weekly schedule for employees can easily be handled through this template.

Weekly Schedule

Period Start Date: Sunday, April 13, 14

Staff	Sun 13	Mon 14	Tue 15	Wed 16
Employee 1 $120 | 8 / 40			7:00 AM - 3:00 PM Front Desk	
Employee 2 $180 | 12 / 40				
Employee 3 $180 | 12 / 40		3:00 PM - 7:00 PM Coordinator		3:00 AM - 7:00 AM Coordinator
Employee 4 $180 | 12 / 40			3:00 PM - 7:00 PM Team Leader	
Employee 5 $120 | 8 / 40	11:00 AM - 3:00 PM Support			
Employee 6 $180 | 12 / 40	3:00 AM - 7:00 AM Coordinator		3:00 AM - 7:00 AM Coordinator	
Employee 7 $60 | 4 / 40				

11. Project Timecard Summary

During the selected time, you can enter the employee rates, names, and hours worked on every project. The worksheet determines each employee's total hours worked as well as the overall hours or labor cost for every project

Weekly Timecard

☐ LOGO

Employee	[Name]
Department	[Department]
Pay Period Starting	11/7/2011
Ending	11/14/2011

[Address 1]
[City, State ZIP]
[Phone]
[Fax]
[Email]

PROJECT	Project Code	Mon	Tue	Wed	Thu	Fri	Sat	Sun	Total Hrs	Overtime Hrs	Regular Hrs
Project Name 1	ABC	5	3.5	2					10.50		10.50
Project Name 2	DEF	3	5.5	6					14.50	3.00	11.50
									0.00		0.00
									0.00		0.00
									0.00		0.00
									0.00		0.00
									0.00		0.00
									0.00		0.00
									0.00		0.00
									0.00		0.00
									0.00		0.00
									0.00		0.00
Holiday									0.00		

12. Company Balance Sheet

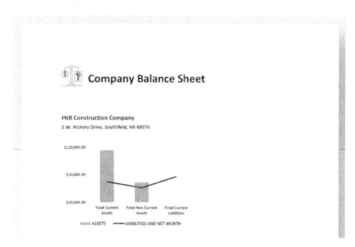

Make a precise representation of the company's actual net worth. This template shows the business's cash, liabilities, and equity at a certain point in time.

13. Weekly Timesheet Template

Weekly Timesheet is a simple template that assists firms and their workers in tracking and monitoring the precise number of work hours worked on a weekly and biweekly basis. The weekly and biweekly timesheets provide a graphical representation of normal hours, overtime, sick

leave, vacation, public holidays, and other events. For your organization, a basic time sheet template may offer a cost-effective time tracking solution. Vertex42.com's timesheet estimates the hours based on a Time In or Time Out, with breaks recorded in minutes. You may divide the hours between regular and overtime as required.

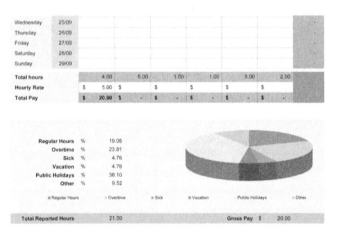

14. Billing Statement

For invoice monitoring, primary consumer account control, and general billing, use this billing statement design.

15. Invoice Tracking

With this template, you can generate and submit invoices using any method you choose. Use PayPal sentences, other templates, or a mix of the two.

16. Cash Flow Statement

Cash Flow Statement
[Company Name]

	For the Year Ending	12/31/2019
	Cash at Beginning of Year	15,700

Operations		
Cash receipts from		
Customers		693,200
Other Operations		
Cash paid for		
Inventory purchases		(264,000)
General operating and administrative expenses		(112,000)
Wage expenses		(123,000)
Interest		(13,500)
Income taxes		(32,800)
Net Cash Flow from Operations		147,900

Investing Activities		
Cash receipts from		
Sale of property and equipment		33,600

Make a list of the company's revenue inflows and outflows. Keep track of where the company's funds come from (cash receipts) and go (cash paid).

17. Price List Template

Using this Excel pricing list template, make a list of the items your firm offers. The retail and bulk pricing columns are included in this professional looking product price list template. Create a price sheet for your items quickly and easily, and organize inventory by product number or description.

LOGO   **PRICE LIST**

Valid From 1-Jan-2014
To 31-Dec-2014

Company Name, Street Address, City, ST ZIP
Phone: (000) 000-0000, Fax: (000) 000-0000, Website: domain.com

Bulk price apply when purchasing the minimum Bulk Qty for that item.

Product Name	Product Number	Description	Unit Price (USD)	Bulk* Qty	Bulk* Unit Price (USD)
Thing One	T001	Description of thing 1	12.00	5	11.00
Thing Two	T002	Description of thing 2	24.00	20	20.50
Thing Three	T003	Description of thing 3	50.00	25	45.00

18. Sales Invoice Template

This invoice template contains all the material you'd expect to send to consumers once they've made a transaction. Make a list of the shipping details, model code, special instructions, and shipping information.

19. Monthly Attendance Checker

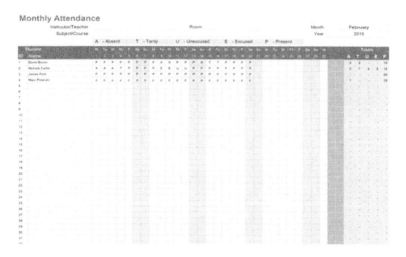

This monthly attendance form example helps you keep track of whether pupils, employees, or team members were active, missing, tardy, or excused.

20. World Meeting Planner

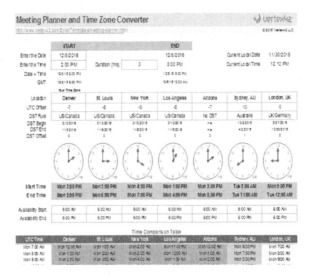

This meeting planner software is designed to help you schedule phone calls and discussions for people who live in various time zones.

21. Fax Cover Sheet

A generic fax cover page is a needed part of faxing that is generally an associated file or document that is sent to your fax.

22. Profit and Loss Statement

The Profit or Loss Account Template is a worthy template for Excel, Google Sheets, and OpenOffice Calc that assists you in quickly preparing your Income Statement. It also allows you to summarize a company's revenues, expenditures, and expenditure over a certain time.

PROFIT AND LOSS

INCOME	Q1	Q1 as % of Sales	Q2	Q2 as % of Sales	Q3	Q3 as % of Sales	Q4	Q4 as % of Sales	Year	Year as % of Sales
Sales Revenue										
Product/Service 1	90.00	52.9%	90.00	52.9%	90.00	52.9%	90.00	52.9%	360.00	52.9%
Product/Service 2	80.00	47.1%	80.00	47.1%	80.00	47.1%	80.00	47.1%	320.00	47.1%
Product/Service 3	-	-	-	-	-	-	-	-	-	-
Product/Service 4	-	-	-	-	-	-	-	-	-	-
Total Sales Revenue	170.00	100.0%	170.00	100.0%	170.00	100.0%	170.00	100.0%	680.00	100.0%
Cost of Sales										
Product/Service 1	100.00	58.8%	100.00	58.8%	100.00	58.8%	100.00	58.8%	400.00	58.8%
Product/Service 2	-	-	-	-	-	-	-	-	-	-
Product/Service 3	-	-	-	-	-	-	-	-	-	-
Product/Service 4	-	-	-	-	-	-	-	-	-	-
Total Cost of Sales	100.00	58.8%	100.00	58.8%	100.00	58.8%	100.00	58.8%	400.00	58.8%
Gross Profit	70.00	41.2%	70.00	41.2%	70.00	41.2%	70.00	41.2%	280.00	41.2%
Non-Operation Income										
Rental	90.00		90.00		90.00		90.00		360.00	
Interest	-		-		-		-		-	
Gifts and Donations Received	-		-		-		-		-	
Other Income (specify)	-		-		-		-		-	
Total Non-Operational Income	90.00		90.00		90.00		90.00		360.00	
TOTAL INCOME	160.00	94.1%	160.00	94.1%	160.00	94.1%	160.00	94.1%	640.00	94.1%

23. Employee Succession Planner

The process by which an organization ensures all employees are recruited & trained to fill each critical function within the firm is known as succession planning. This procedure ensures that you'll never have a critical position vacant for which another person is unprepared.

24. Simple Balance Sheet

Create finance balance reports with the help of this financial professional-made blueprint. Anything that needs to be considered is covered.

25. Annual Sales Report

Determine which aspects of your business contribute to your performance, and protect your company's future growth for the coming year.

26. Milestone Chart

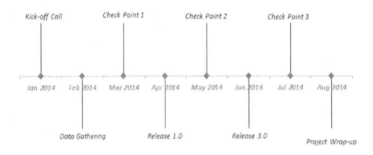

As critical as the project itself is a determination to executing. A milestone chart is a valuable method for illustrating the scale and timelines of a project.

27. Manufacturing Business Accounting

Accounting System for Manufacturing Enterprises is an Excel spreadsheet that can be used to record and generate financial reports for manufacturing companies. A manufacturing business acquires raw materials and transforms them into marketable finished items.

		BS FORMAT	BS REPORT 1	BS REPORT 2	BS REPORT 3		Click on "+"
HOME				BALANCE SHEET			
				For The Year Ended janv, d yyyy			
SETUP		Select CoA Code Below		Fill Initial Data Below			
ORDER		Account No	Account Name	01/01/17 Balance	30/01/17 Balance		*Monthly F available in
			ASSETS				
JOURNAL			Current Assets				
		1110	CASH - Petty Cash		200,00	v	Type "v" fo
		1120	CASH - Operating Account	700,00	196,65	v	rows (Cash,
INVENTORY		1130	Central Bank	1 727,50	3 061,50	v	will be usec
		1250	Account Receivables	1 534,35	6 396,60		Cash Flow f
		1310	Raw Materials Inventory	6 300,00	2 000,00		
BALANCE SHEET		1320	Work in Progress Inventory	0,00	500,00		
		1330	Finished Goods Inventory	300,00	4 151,67		
		1360	Office Inventory	600,00	591,00		
PROFIT & LOSS		1410	PREPAID - Insurance		(25,00)		
		1420	PREPAID - Rent		(50,00)		
CASH FLOW							
EQUITY			Fixed Assets				
		1510	PPE - Computer Equipment	500,00	900,00		
CoGM		1620	ACCUM DEPR - Machinery and Equipment	-75,00	(227,92)		
		1540	PPE - Vehicles	6 000,00	6 000,00		
		1640	ACCUM DEPR - Vehicles	-500,00	(550,00)		
OTHER							

28. SWOT Chart

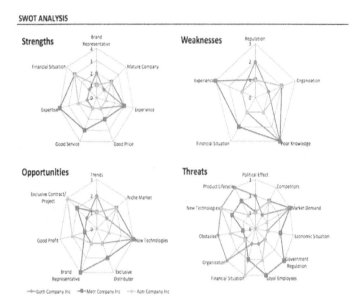

Prepare for the introduction of a new product in advance. SWOT analysis may be used to assess its place among existing companies in the sector (strengths, threats, weaknesses, opportunities).

29. Year-End Inventory Analysis

The ultimate value of items held by a corporation at the conclusion of a financial period, like the accounting year, is referred to as ending inventory. Value of ending inventory is determined by subtracting a cost of items sold out from the value of starting inventory. Inventory must be reported on your tax return to calculate your revenue and loss for the year. You must calculate your cost of products sold in more detail (COGS). This is the cost of the objects or materials used in their production (like cost of buying and manufacturing inventory).

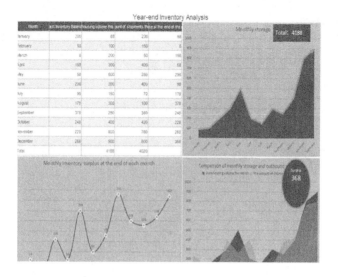

30. Bill of Sale (General Form)

It is a legal document supplied by a seller to a purchaser as just a descriptive material describing the purchaser's complete payment to the seller for the acquired item and serving as a receipt or evidence to avoid any obligation.

BILL SALE (General Form)

In consideration of the sum of $ _____ the receipt of which is hereby acknowledged, the undersigned, SELLER, hereby sells, assigns and transfers to _____, BUYER, the following personal property:

(Description)

SELLER warrants it has good title to said property, free and clear of all encumbrances, and has full authority to assign and transfer the same, and warrants that it will defend and indemnify the BUYER from any and all claims to said property.

31. Digital Marketing Strategy

Setting marketing objectives based on market research and target audiences, choosing digital marketing channels as well as platforms, ascertaining channel-specific delivery strategies, or specifying macro marketing to measure the digital marketing strategy's performance are all part of a digital marketing strategy.

32. Background Check Form

It is a summary of an employee's professional life, including educational qualifications, previous employment history, and family information. It is often requested by employers to complete at the time of hire or before to hire in order to check the employee's background. Some companies may include a section for criminal record clarification.

33. Dynamic Pareto Chart

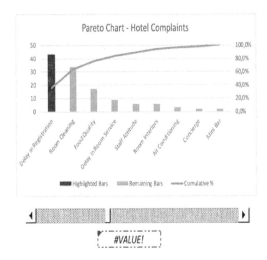

The Pareto theory (also known as the 80/20 rule) is a well-known theory in project management, and the Pareto Chart is founded on it. This template will enable you to quickly incorporate it into your spreadsheets.

34. Payment Schedule Sample Form

The payment template is a set of instructions which you may use to make payments or collect money on a regular basis. Templates make it simple to create and utilize recurring payments, such as: Vendor and supplier payments. Customers' collections.

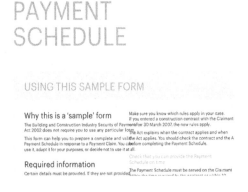

35. Simple Personal Budget

The personal budget template from Excel might help you better understand your money. Personal budgeting templates assist you in keeping track of your monthly income and spending. Sparklines reveal patterns and trends in your expenditure by calculating monthly and annual totals.

36. To-Do List With Priorities

A prioritized To Do list is a basic list that you may use to keep track of the chores you need to do each day. This template helps you to keep track of all the tasks you want to undertake on a given day and prioritize them.

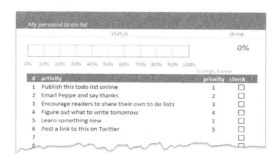

37. General Analysis Charts

This template can be used for analyzing different chart types and data from different sources in form of chart type.

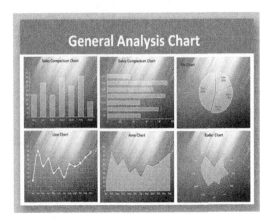

38. Automated Emails

Excel automation makes it easier to use the program by automating operations like cell formatting, changing data, and executing macros. You may also combine Excel jobs in automated processes with the other jobs throughout the organization using an RPA system. We were able to quickly design a flow which sends emails depending on data in an Excel table that was attached. Microsoft Flow is for you if you can use a mouse or have some ideas for procedures you'd want to automate.

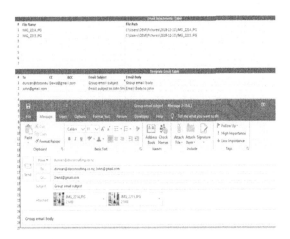

39. Conference and Meeting Agenda

The agenda is a copy of the meeting plan that is sent to participants. A meeting agenda can comprise a list of subjects to discuss, a schedule of actions to be completed, or both. For each agenda item, formal agendas will contain time and presenter information.

1 Day Conference on something awesome

Start time: 1/4/2013 10:00 AM

#	Activity Detail	Start Time	Duration (minutes)	End Time
1	Presentation 1	10:00 AM	60 mins	11:00 AM
2	Presentation 2	11:00 AM	30 mins	11:30 AM
3	Presentation 3	11:30 AM	30 mins	12:00 PM
4	Break	12:00 PM	20 mins	12:20 PM
5	Presentation 4	12:20 PM	45 mins	01:05 PM
6	Presentation 5	01:05 PM	30 mins	01:35 PM
7	Presentation 6	01:35 PM	15 mins	01:50 PM

40. Simple Contract

The certainty of the phrases, as well as their meaning, show that Michael was confident of purchasing the automobile for $800.00, whereas Boris was confident of selling his automobile to Michael for $800.00. As a result, both parties were clear in their transactions, resulting in a straightforward contract.

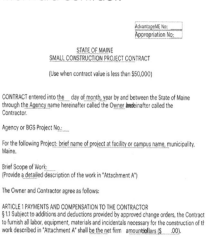

41. Break-Even Analysis

Break-even analysis is the examination of how many sales or units must be sold to break even after all fixed and variable expenses are considered. Break-even analysis helps businesses figure out how many units they need to sell to pay all of their expenses and start making money.

42. Credit Memo

A credit note is a document that a vendor of goods or services sends to a customer alerting them of the amount they owe the vendor. You'll need a credit or debit memo to hand out to consumers if you're in the industry of supplying products or services.

43. Sales Receipt

To offer complete payment information to consumers, use Excel's standard blue sales receipt. Taxes, discounts, unit pricing, subtotals, and other data are structured in this sales receipt.

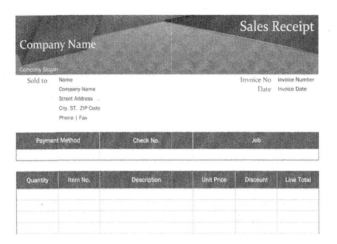

44. Fishbone Diagram

Fishbone diagrams show all the possible mistakes and reasons that might affect the system and your job. The result is usually a problem, and the reasons are documented and organized to assist venture management in preventing the situation. Because of its form, a fishbone diagram excel is referred to as a fishbone.

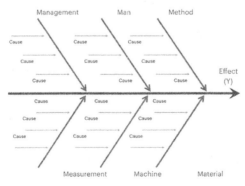

45. Employee Training Tracker

Employee Training Tracker is also an Excel Spreadsheet that is used to keep track of the company's training programs. This form may be used to keep track of staff training and budgets. You'll be able to keep track of learning programs and plan your team's progress using this template.

46. Critical Path Analysis

The longest route in the precedence diagram you produced is referred to as the critical route. You must first determine how long each of the various pathways will take to finish before you can calculate the crucial path. The SUMPRODUCT function in Excel might help you with this.

Critical Path Analysis: Examples

Question 1

The precedence table for activities involved in producing a computer game is shown opposite.

An activity on arc network is to be drawn to model this production process.

a Explain why it is necessary to use at least two dummies when drawing the activity network

b Draw the activity network using exactly two dummies.

Activity	Must be preceded by
A	—
B	—
C	B
D	A, C
E	A
F	E
G	E
H	G
I	D, F
J	G, I
K	G, I
L	H, K

47. Timeline Editing

When you pick the timeline inside the worksheet, this tab displays in the Ribbon. The buttons on this page are used to change the timeline parameters in Excel or make other alterations to the timeline. The "Timeline" button is located at the tab's left end.

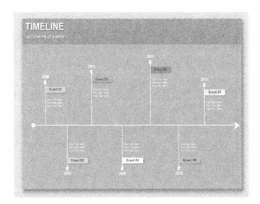

48. Sales Funnel Chart

Funnel charts depict values at various phases of a process. A funnel chart, for example, might be used to represent the number of sales prospects at every step of a sales pipeline.

Funnel Stage	Value (in $ 000s)	Funnel Visualization	Conv %
Initial contact	$ 13,210		
Application of Initial Fit Criteria	$ 8,250		⬇ 62%
Sales lead	$ 7,400		⬇ 90%
Need identification	$ 6,200		⬇ 84%
Qualified prospect	$ 4,847		⬇ 78%
Proposal	$ 3,215		⬇ 66%
Negotiation	$ 2,020		⬇ 63%
Closing	$ 963		⬇ 48%
Deal Transaction	$ 904		⬇ 94%

Chapter 7: Relative, Absolute, and Mixed Cell References in Excel

In Excel, a worksheet is made up of cells. By defining the row and column values, these cells may be referred to. A1 refers to the first row (specified as 1) and the first column (specified as A). B3 corresponds to the third row and second column. Excel's strength resides in the idea that you can use specific cell references in calculations in other cells.

In Excel, you will now use three different types of cell references:

- Mixed cell references
- Relative cell references
- Absolute cell references

Understanding the various forms of cell references can aid you in formula work and save you time (particularly when copy-pasting the formulas).

7.1 What Are Relative Cell References in Excel?

To demonstrate the principle of relative cell references in Excel, you'll use a basic illustration. Assume you have the following data set:

	A	B	C	D
1	Item	Price	Quantity	Total
2	Item A	15	15	
3	Item B	20	20	
4	Item C	12	18	
5	Item D	18	8	
6	Item E	8	10	
7	Item F	10	20	
8	Item G	20	10	

To figure out the sum for each object, add the price by the amount of that item. The formula in cell D2 for the first item will be B2*C2 (as seen below):

	A	B	C	D
1	Item	Price	Quantity	Total
2	Item A	15	15	225
3	Item B	20	20	
4	Item C	12	18	
5	Item D	18	8	
6	Item E	8	10	
7	Item F	10	20	
8	Item G	20	10	

D2 fx =B2*C2

You will now copy cell D2 and insert it into all the other cells instead of entering the formula for each cell one by one (D3:D8). You'll see that the cell relation immediately adjusts to apply to the corresponding row as you do so. e.g., in cell D3, the formula becomes B3*C3, and in cell D4, the formula becomes B4*C4.

7.1.1 When to Use Relative Cell References in Excel?

When you try to build a method for several cells and the formula must link to a relative cell relation, relative cell comparisons are helpful. You will build the formula for one cell and copy-paste it into all cells in this scenario.

7.2 What are Absolute Cell References in Excel?

Unlike relative cell references, absolute cell comparisons do not alter as the formula is copied to other cells. Assume you have the data collection shown below, then you need to figure out the commission on each item's gross revenue. The commission is 20%, and It's seen in cell G1.

	A	B	C	D	E	F	G
1	Item	Price	Quantity	Total	Commission		20%
2	Item A	15	15	225			
3	Item B	20	20	400			
4	Item C	12	18	216			
5	Item D	18	8	144			
6	Item E	8	10	80			
7	Item F	10	20	200			
8	Item G	20	10	200			

Using the following formula in cell E2 and copy it for all cells to get the commission number for each item sale:

=D2*G1

Focus on two-dollar signs ($) in the cell reference that has the commission—G2.

7.2.1 What Does The Dollar ($) Sign Do?

When a dollar sign is placed in front of a row or column number, it becomes absolute.

As I copy the formula from cell E2 to cell E3, it switches from =D2*G1 to =D3*G1. It's worth noting that, while D2 becomes D3, G1 remains unchanged. Since we put a dollar sign in front of "G" and "1" in G1, the cell reference wouldn't shift when we copied it. As a result, the cell relation is now absolute.

7.2.2 When to Use Absolute Cell References in Excel?

When you don't want the cell relation to shifting as you copy formulas, absolute cell references are helpful. If you have a constant variable that you ought to include in a calculation, this may be the case (such as commission

rate, tax rate, number of months, etc.) Although you might need complex code this meaning in the formula (e.g., G2 instead of 20%), putting it in a cell and only using the cell relation helps you adjust it later. If the commission structure shifts, for example, and you now payout 25% instead of 20%, you will quickly adjust the value in cell G2, and all the calculations can update automatically.

7.3 What Are Mixed Cell References in Excel?

Absolute and relative cell comparisons are easier to work with than mixed cell references. Mixed cell references may be of two types:

- When the formula is copied, the row is locked when the column shifts.
- When the formula is copied, the column is locked when the row changes.

Let's look at a scenario and see how it functions. You must measure the three tiers of commission depending on the percentage values in cells E2, F2, and G2 in the data set below.

	A	B	C	D	E	F	G
1						Commission	
2					10%	15%	20%
3	Item	Price	Quantity	Total	Tier 1	Tier 2	Tier 3
4	Item A	15	15	225			
5	Item B	20	20	400			
6	Item C	12	18	216			
7	Item D	18	8	144			
8	Item E	8	10	80			
9	Item F	10	20	200			
10	Item G	20	10	200			

You can now measure both commissions with only one calculation, thanks to the strength of mixed reference. Copy the formula below into cell E4 and all other cells.

=$B4*$C4*E$2

E4 fx =$B4*$C4*E$2

	A	B	C	D	E	F	G
1						Commission	
2					10%	15%	20%
3	Item	Price	Quantity	Total	Tier 1	Tier 2	Tier 3
4	Item A	15	15	225	22.5	33.75	45
5	Item B	20	20	400	40	60	80
6	Item C	12	18	216	21.6	32.4	43.2
7	Item D	18	8	144	14.4	21.6	28.8
8	Item E	8	10	80	8	12	16
9	Item F	10	20	200	20	30	40
10	Item G	20	10	200	20	30	40

Both types of mixed cell references are included in the formula above (one where the row is locked and where the column is locked). Let's look at each cell reference to see how it works:

- $B4 (& $C4)—The dollar sign appears earlier than the Column notation but not before the Row number in this example. Since the column is set, the relation would stay the same as you copy a formula to the cells on the right. This relation does not alter if you copied the formula from E4 to F4. However, when it is not closed, the row number can shift as you copy it down.
- E$2—The dollar sign appears just before the row number in this example, and there is no dollar sign in the column notation. Since the row number is locked, the relation would not shift when you copy a formula down the cells. However, since the formula is not locked, the column alphabet would shift if you copied it to the right.

7.4 How to Change the Reference From Relative to Absolute (or Mixed)?

You must add the dollar sign even before column notation and the row number to shift the relation from relative to absolute. A1 is a relative cell relation, so it becomes absolute when you change it to A1.

If you need to modify a couple of references, you can find it simple to do so manually. So, you may edit the formula in the formula bar (or select the cell, press F2, and then change it). However, utilizing the keyboard shortcut—F4—is a more straightforward way to do this. As you click F4 when selecting a cell reference (in the formula bar or edit mode), the reference is changed.

Consider the case where you have the relation =A1 in a cell.

When you pick the relation and click the F4 key, this is what happens.

After you've pressed the F4 key, do the following: The cell relation shifts from A1 to A1 (from "relative" to "absolute").

Press the F4 key twice to shift the cell relation from A1 to A$1 (changes to mixed reference where the row is locked).

Three times press the F4 key: A1 becomes $A1 as the cell index (changes to mixed reference where the column is locked).

Press the F4 key four times to change the cell relation back to A1.

7.4.1 Create Multiplication Table in Excel and Google Sheets

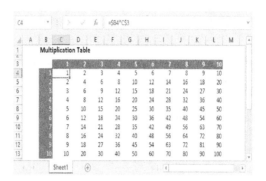

7.4.2 Setting Up Data

To set up the data, enter the numbers 1–10 in cells A2 to A11 and again in cells B1 to K1.

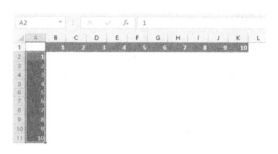

With the TRANSPOSE feature, you can even insert numbers in the cells in an interesting way:

1. In cells A2 to A11, write the numbers 1–10.
2. In the formula bar, type the following formula for the range B1:K1.
3. Since this is an array formula, press Ctrl +Shift +Enter

=TRANSPOSE (A2:A11)

7.5 Multiplication Table Using Mixed References

Mixed cell references, in which one row or column reference is locked and the other is not, may construct a multiplication table. Use this formula in cell B2:

=$A2*B$1

This locks the header row for the total, multiplies the header column row, and returns the result. Then we'll copy and paste the following formula in the range:

1. Ctrl + C to copy cell B2.
2. Choose the B2:K11 set.

3. To paste the formula, press Ctrl +V.

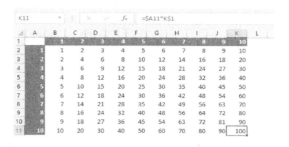

7.6 Multiplication Table Using an Array Formula

The array formula approach is indeed very straightforward. Simply pick the set B1:K1 and type the formula in the formula bar, then click Ctrl +Shift+ Enter

=A2:A11*B1:K1

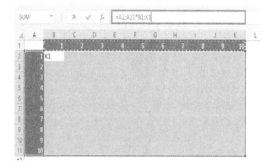

The complete multiplication table will be made by using this way.

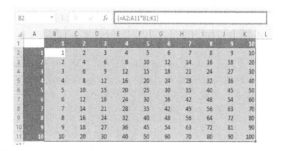

89

7.7 Create the Multiplication Table in Google Sheets

The formula for creating the multiplication table works precisely, in the same way, like in Google Sheets as in Excel:

	1	2	3	4	5	6	7	8	9	10
1	1	2	3	4	5	6	7	8	9	10
2	2	4	6	8	10	12	14	16	18	20
3	3	6	9	12	15	18	21	24	27	30
4	4	8	12	16	20	24	28	32	36	40
5	5	10	15	20	25	30	35	40	45	50
6	6	12	18	24	30	36	42	48	54	60
7	7	14	21	28	35	42	49	56	63	70
8	8	16	24	32	40	48	56	64	72	80
9	9	18	27	36	45	54	63	72	81	90
10	10	20	30	40	50	60	70	80	90	100

7.8 Numbering in Excel

When working in Excel, there are a few minor things that may be completed repeatedly, and if we know how to perform them correctly, we will save a lot of time. Creating numbers in Excel is a job that is often performed at work. In Excel, serial numbers are incredibly significant. This gives each record in your spreadsheet a distinct identity. One method is to manually enter the serial numbers into Excel. However, whether you have hundreds or thousands of rows of data to insert the row number with, it may be a headache.

7.8.1 How to Automatically Add a Serial Number in Excel?

In Excel, there are many methods for calculating the number of rows:

1. **Using the Fill Handle**

This quickly detects a trend from a few already filled cells and applies it to the whole column. Have a look at the set below.

	A	B	C	D	E	F
1						
2	Serial No.	Store	Product A	Product B	Product C	
3	1	Store A	64	53	88	
4	2	Store B	49	27	82	
5	3	Store C	18	22	61	
6	4	Store D	38	29	90	
7	5	Store E	29	90	22	
8	6	Store F	67	83	29	
9	7	Store G	45	67	42	
10	8	Store H	58	58	68	
11	9	Store I	27	31	37	
12	10	Store J	81	36	25	
13	11	Store K	56	35	15	
14	12	Store L	38	19	84	
15	13	Store M	14	36	42	
16						

Follow the measures below:

1. In cell A3, write 1, and in Cell A4, write 2.
2. Choose all cells as seen in the screenshot given below.

	A	B	C	D	E	F
1						
2	Serial No.	Store	Product A	Product B	Product C	
3	1	Store A	64	53	88	
4	2	Store B	49	27	82	
5		Store C	18	22	61	
6		Store D	38	29	90	
7		Store E	29	90	22	
8		Store F	67	83	29	
9		Store G	45	67	42	
10		Store H	58	58	68	
11		Store I	27	31	37	
12		Store J	81	36	25	
13		Store K	56	35	15	
14		Store L	38	19	84	
15		Store M	14	36	42	
16						

3. As shown in the above screenshot, there is a tiny square rounded in red labeled Fill Handle in Excel. Double-click on the fill handle with the mouse cursor on this square. It will occupy all the cells before the dataset is finished. Have a look at the image below.

The template is identified by the fill handle, which then fills the appropriate cells with that pattern. If the dataset contains some blank rows, the fill handle would only run until the last contiguous non-blank segment.

2. Making Use of Full Series

This idea makes more control over data on how the serial numbers can enter the excel. Assume you have below the score of all students' subject-wise.

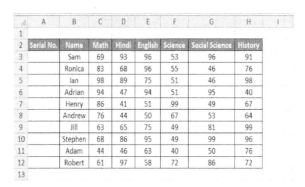

To fill series in Excel, follow the steps below:

1. In Cell A3, type 1.
2. Choose the HOME key. As seen in the screenshot below, go to the editing section and select the Fill option.

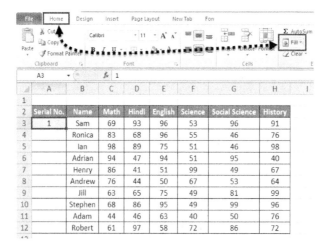

3. Choose Fill from the dropdown menu. It has a lot of choices. As seen in the screenshot below, choose Series.

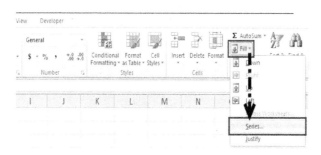

4. It will open another dialog box as given below.

5. Press on the columns under the series in section.

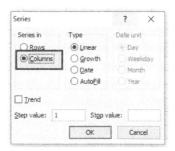

6. In the Stop Value area, type the value. We have a limit of 10 records in this case; enter 10. The Fill Series alternative will not function if you leave this value blank.
7. Click the OK button. Rows of serial numbers ranging from 1 to 10 would be filled because of this. Have a look at the image below.

	A	B	C	D	E	F	G	H	I
1									
2	Serial No.	Name	Math	Hindi	English	Science	Social Science	History	
3	1	Sam	69	93	96	53	96	91	
4	2	Ronica	83	68	96	55	46	76	
5	3	Ian	98	89	75	51	46	98	
6	4	Adrian	94	47	94	51	95	40	
7	5	Henry	86	41	51	99	49	67	
8	6	Andrew	76	44	50	67	53	64	
9	7	Jill	63	65	75	49	81	99	
10	8	Stephen	68	86	95	49	99	96	
11	9	Adam	44	46	63	40	50	76	
12	10	Robert	61	97	58	72	86	72	
13									

3. Using the ROW Function

In Excel, there is a built-in feature that can be utilized to number the rows. Enter the following formula in the first cell to obtain the excel row numbering.

	A	B	C	D	E	F
1						
2						
3	Serial No.	Store	Product A	Product B	Product C	
4		Store A	64	53	88	
5		Store B	49	27	82	
6		Store C	18	22	61	
7		Store D	38	29	90	
8		Store E	29	90	22	
9		Store F	67	83	29	
10		Store G	45	67	42	
11		Store H	58	58	68	
12		Store I	27	31	37	
13		Store J	81	36	25	
14		Store K	56	35	15	
15		Store L	38	19	84	
16		Store M	14	36	42	
17						

The ROW feature returns the current row's excel row total. If the data begins on the second row, deduct one.
Look at the image below. Using the formula =ROW()-3

OFFSET		✗ ✓ fx	=ROW()-3			
	A	B	C	D	E	F
1						
2						
3	Serial No.	Store	Product A	Product B	Product C	
4	=ROW()-3	Store A	64	53	88	
5		Store B	49	27	82	
6		Store C	18	22	61	
7		Store D	38	29	90	
8		Store E	29	90	22	
9		Store F	67	83	29	
10		Store G	45	67	42	
11		Store H	58	58	68	
12		Store I	27	31	37	
13		Store J	81	36	25	
14		Store K	56	35	15	
15		Store L	38	19	84	
16		Store M	14	36	42	
17						

Drag the formula for the rest of the rows, and the result is given below:

Tips About Numbering in Excel

- Fill Handle and Fill Series are all fixed options.

- The row number would remain unchanged whether you pass or erase some record or row in the dataset.

- If you cut and copy the data in Excel, the ROW feature provides you the exact counting.

Chapter 8: MS Excel: The WORKDAY.INTL Function

The WORKDAY.INTL feature belongs to the Excel Date and Time functions category. It's a more versatile version of the WORKDAY feature since it deals with weekend criteria that can be customized. WORKDAY.INTL can supply us with a date on N working days in the past or the future, allowing us to decide weekend times. The feature may also be used to add or remove days from a specified date.

The WORKDAY.INTL function may be used in financial analysis to calculate the number of workdays worked by workers, due payment dates, estimated arrival period for an order, or a debtor aging plan. The most valuable benefit is that we let go tailor weekends, allowing us to do it in various countries for different weekends.

The formula is as shown below:

=WORKDAY.INTL(start_date, days, [weekend], [holidays])

- **Start date (required function)**—This is a date that indicates the beginning of the process.

Weekend number	Weekend days
1 or omitted	Saturday, Sunday
2	Sunday, Monday
3	Monday, Tuesday

4	Tuesday, Wednesday
5	Wednesday, Thursday
6	Thursday, Friday
7	Friday, Saturday
11	Sunday only
12	Monday only
13	Tuesday only
14	Wednesday only
15	Thursday only
16	Friday only
17	Saturday only

- **Days (mandatory function)**—The number of working days to apply to the start date. A favorable outcome would result in a potential day, while a negative value will result in a past date.
- **Weekend (selectable argument)**—This specifies the week's days are designated as weekends and cannot be called working days. A weekend is a number or series that indicates when weekends take place. The weekend number values show the following weekend days:

- **Weekend string**—This is a string of seven 0's and 1's that starts with Monday and reflects the seven days of the week. A non-working day is represented by 1, and a working day is represented by 0. Include the after scenario:
    - "0000011"—Weekends are Saturday and Sunday.
    - "1000001" – days are Monday and Sunday.
- **[Holidays] (optional argument)**—Several dates that aren't considered workdays. The list may either be an array constant of serial numbers that show the dates or a set of cells that include the dates. Times or serial values in holidays may be ordered in any sequence.

When entering times, Microsoft suggests using the following syntax for the start date and [holidays] arguments:

1. Cells representing dates are referenced.
2. The dates the formulas return.

If we enter date claims as text, there's a chance Excel will misrepresent them, based on your computer's date scheme and date representation settings.

8.1 How to Use a WORKDAY.INTL Function in Excel?

The WORKDAY feature first appeared in Excel 2007 and has since been added to all subsequent versions of Excel. Find the following scenario to better explain the function's applications:

As an example:

Let's say we want to allocate 30 days to one workday and deduct 20 days from another. Friday and Saturday are the weekends in this town. The formula was as follows:

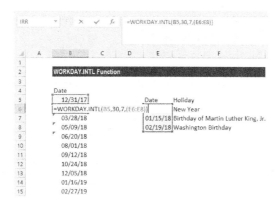

Holidays are described here as the called set holidays (E6:E8), but holidays are often considered.

Excel just cares for dates, not what day of the week it is. That is, it is unconcerned about the holiday's real name.

The below are the outcomes:

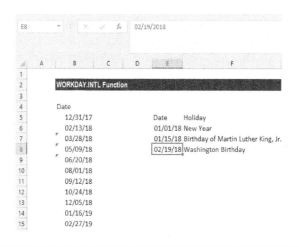

8.2 WORKDAY.INTL Errors

8.2.1 Mistake #NUM

Occurs when:

- The specified day's statement and the provided start date result in an invalid date; or
- The weekend point is a nonsensical argument.
- The days given would be truncated if they are not integers.
- Dates are stored in MS Excel as sequential serial numbers, allowing them to be used in calculations. Since it is 43,101 days after January 1, 1900, serial number 1 is assigned by default, and serial number 43101 is assigned by default.

8.2.2 #VALUE Error

This error appears when:

- The assigned start date and all the [holidays] array's values are not valid dates.
- The day's claim is not a number.
- The [weekend] statement is a text string that is not true.

8.3 MS Excel: The RANDBETWEEN Function

The RANDBETWEEN Function is classified as a Math and Trigonometry function in Excel. Between the user-specified values, the function will return a random integer number. Any time the worksheet is opened or computed; it will return a random integer number.

A financial analyst may use the RANDBETWEEN function to produce random integer numbers within a given range. However, like other disciplines such as cryptography and statistics, it is used less commonly in the finance industry.

The formula is:

= RANDBETWEEN (bottom, top)

1. Bottom (necessary function)—This is the function's smallest integer return value.
2. Top (necessary function)—This is the function's highest integer return value.

8.4 How to Use the RANDBETWEEN Function in Excel?

Consider the following scenario to further explain the RANDBETWEEN function:

As an example:

Any time the worksheet is measured or opened, we can get different results if we enter data in the Bottom and Top columns below:

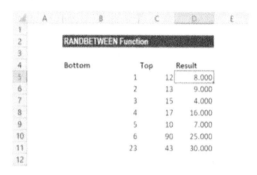

=RANDBETWEEN (B5, C5) was the formula used

The worksheet modified the outcome when we did some recalculations, as seen below:

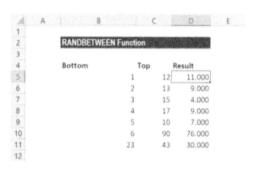

8.5 Tips for the RANDBETWEEN Function

- Every time the worksheet is computed, RANDBETWEEN can generate a new value. To prevent random numbers from being generated, copy the cells containing RANDBETWEEN to

101

the clipboard and convert them to text using Paste Special > Values.
- Insert the RANDBETWEEN feature in the Formulas bar and then click F9 to transform the formula into its result if we choose a random number that would not alter until the worksheet is computed.
- To create a collection of random numbers in multiple cells, select the cells, use the RANDBETWEEN tool, and then press Ctrl + Enter.

8.6 Excel RAND Function

To generate random numbers in Excel, use the RAND function. Then, for arranging or retrieving records from a table, use a column of random numbers. Using the following method to generate a random number in a cell:

RAND= ()

Using the RAND feature to delegate numbers or assignments to a set of people at random. There are five individuals in this case, as well as the numbers 1–25.

1. Begin typing the list of people's names in cell A1.
2. Choose any of the names and transfer the cursor to the bottom right corner's fill handle.

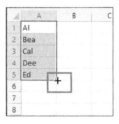

3. Drag down to row 25 as the cursor switches to a black plus symbol. The name sequence would be repeated down the column because of this.

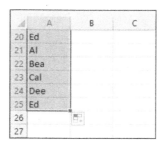

4. Leave column B empty.
5. Begin in cell C1 by making a list of numbers or activities that will be allocated at random.
6. NOTE: To make a sequential list of numbers, enter the first two numbers, pick them, and drag them down to row 25.

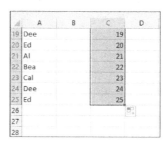

7. In the cell D1, type the RAND formula for creating a random number. "=RAND ()"

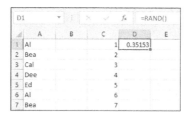

8. Fill up the RAND formula all the way to row 25.
9. Then, in the popup menu, right-click on the number in D1:D25 & choose Sort, then Sort Smallest to Largest.

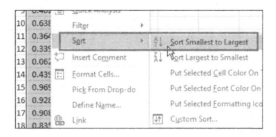

10. Finally, remove column D (RAND formulas) and column B (the vacant column) from the list of 1 to 25 names.
11. Per name has a randomly allocated number from the list of 1 to 25 names.

	A	B	C
1	Al	12	
2	Bea	18	
3	Cal	13	
4	Dee	2	
5	Ed	19	
6	Al	7	
7	Bea	21	
8	Cal	9	
9	Dee	17	
10	Ed	10	

8.6.1 Create Random Numbers

1. Use month headings, consumer numbers, and random numbers to quickly generate test results, then change the formulas to static values.
2. Make a random text and number generator
3. To generate random numbers in Excel, use the RANDBETWEEN function.

Chapter 9: MS Excel: The VLOOKUP Function

The VLOOKUP feature in Excel allows you to look up a specific piece of data in a table or data collection and retrieve the associated data/information. In plain English, the VLOOKUP feature tells Excel to 'look for this piece of information (e.g., bananas) in this data collection (a table) and tell me any corresponding information about it (e.g., banana price)."

The formula is:

=VLOOKUP (lookup value, table array, col index num, [range lookup])

To put it another way, the formula says, "Find this piece of information in the following field and send me some matching details from another column." The following arguments are passed to the VLOOKUP function:

1. Lookup value (necessary argument)—Lookup value defines the value in the first column of a table that we want to look up.
2. Table array (necessary argument)—The table array represents the data array to be scanned. The VLOOKUP feature looks in the array's left-most column.
3. Col index num (necessary argument)—This is an integer that specifies the column number of the supplied table array from which a value should be returned.
4. Range lookup (selectable argument)—This specifies what this feature can return if it cannot locate an exact match for the lookup value. The value of the statement may be TRUE or FALSE, which means:
- **TRUE**—Estimated match, which means that the nearest match below the lookup value is used if an exact match cannot be sought.

- **FALSE**—Exact match; if an exact match is not detected, an error would be returned.

9.1 How to Use VLOOKUP in Excel?

9.1.1 Sort the Information

The first step in utilizing the VLOOKUP feature is to ensure your data is well-organized and appropriate for it. Since VLOOKUP operates from left to right, you must ensure that the data you wish to look up is to the left of the data you want to extract. e.g.

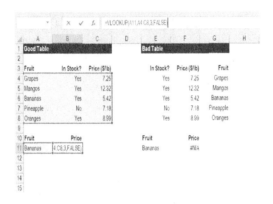

Since bananas are in the leftmost column in the above VLOOKUP illustration, the "healthy table" will quickly run the function to look up "Bananas" and return their price. There is an error message in the "bad table" case because the columns are not in the correct sequence. This is one of VLOOKUP's most significant flaws, and It's for this purpose, INDEX MATCH can be used instead of VLOOKUP.

9.1.2 What to Lookup, Tell the Function

We say Excel what to see for in this process. First, type the formula =VLOOKUP ("and select a cell comprising the data we want to look up. It's the cell that says "Bananas" in this situation.

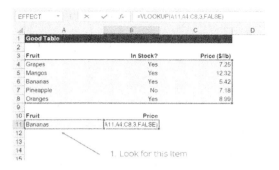

9.1.3 Tell the Function Where to Look

In this stage, we select the table containing the data and instruct Excel to look for the details we choose in the previous phase in the leftmost column. In this example, we've highlighted the entire table from column A to column C. Excel would search in column A for the details we told it to look up.

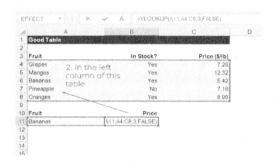

9.1.4 Tell Excel What Column to Output the Data From

We must say Excel, which column contains the data we want to provide as an output from the VLOOKUP. Excel would require a number that correlates to the table's column number. Since the output data is in the third column of the table in our case, we use the number "3" in the formula.

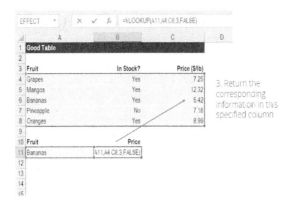

9.1.5 Approximate or Same Exact Match

By entering "False" or "True" in the formula, you can say Excel if you're searching for an exact or estimated match. We want the same or exact match ("Bananas") in our VLOOKUP function formula example, so we typeface "False" in the formula. We might get a close match if we used "True" as a factor instead.

When looking up an actual statistic that isn't in the table, for example, the number 2.9585, an estimated match will be helpful. Excel can search for the nearest to 2.9585 in this situation, even though that number isn't in the dataset. This would help avoid VLOOKUP formula errors.

9.2 VLOOKUP in Financial Modeling and Financial Analysis

VLOOKUP formulas are often used in financial modeling and other forms of financial analysis to render simulations more complex and integrate different examples.

Consider a financial model that contained a debt plan and three alternative interest rate scenarios: 3.0 percent, 4.0 percent, and 5.0 percent. A VLOOKUP could look for a low, medium, or high scenario and then output the associated interest rate into the financial model.

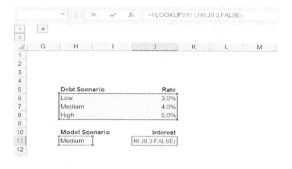

9.3 Tips for the VLOOKUP Function

The following is a set of essential items to note regarding the Excel VLOOKUP Function:

1. The VLOOKUP feature would allow a non-exact match if range lookup is omitted, but it would use an exact match if one existed.
2. The function's most significant flaw is that it still seems to be right. It can pull data from the columns to the right of the table's first node.
3. VLOOKUP can only fit the first value if the lookup column includes redundant values.
4. The role is unaffected by the situation.
5. Assume that a VLOOKUP formula already exists in a worksheet. In that case, if we add a column to the table, formulas will split. Since hard-coded column index values do not adjust immediately as columns are added or removed, this is the case.
6. Wildcards, such as an asterisk (*) or a question mark (?), may be used for VLOOKUP.
7. Assume the table we're dealing with has numbers inserted as text in the function. It doesn't matter whether we're only extracting numbers as text from a table panel. However, if the table's first column includes numbers entered as text, we'll get a #N/A! If the lookup value is not indeed in text type, an error will occur.
8. #NONE. If the VLOOKUP function fails to locate a fit for the supplied lookup value, an error is returned.
9. #REF Error – Occurs whenever one or more of the following conditions are met:

- The number of columns in the supplied table array is greater than the col index num argument; or
- The formula tried to appeal to cells that did not function.
10. #WORTH. Error—Occurs whenever one or more of the following conditions are met:
    - The col_index num statement is less than one or isn't a numeric value; or
    - The range_lookup statement isn't understood as a TRUE or FALSE logical value.

9.3.1 VLOOKUP and #N/A Errors

If you use VLOOKUP, you'll almost certainly get a #N/A warning. The error code #N/A simply indicates "not identified." All the three VLOOKUP formulas return back into #N/A if the lookup cost or value for "Toy Story 2" did not appear in the lookup table on the screen given below:

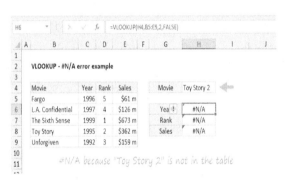

One method to "trap" the N/A error is to use the IFNA function like below:

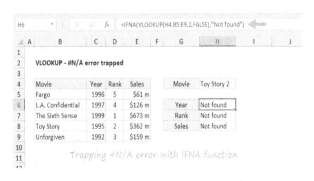

H6 shows the formula which is = IFNA and i.e., (VLOOKUP (H4, B5; E9, 2, FALSE), "Not found")

This error will tell you:

- The lookup formula is misspelled or includes extra space in the table.
- Match mode is the same rather than should be approximate
- The table set is not inserted correctly
- Copy the VLOOKUP, and the table relation is not locked.

9.4 MS Excel: the HLOOKUP Function

Horizontal Lookup is the abbreviation for HLOOKUP, and it is used to extract data from a table by scanning a row for similar data and then outputting the results from the corresponding section. HLOOKUP looks for a value in a row, while VLOOKUP looks for a value in a column.

The formula is:

= HLOOKUP (value to look up, table area, row number).

9.5 How to Use the HLOOKUP Function in Excel?

Consider the following scenario. The below are the grades for four subjects for five students:

	A	B	C	D	E	F
Student name	A	B	C	D	E	
Accounts		75	65	70	60	59
Economics		65	72	78	89	67
Management		70	68	90	72	58
Mathematics		80	90	75	65	87

We can use the HLOOKUP function as given below after fetching the marks of student D in management.

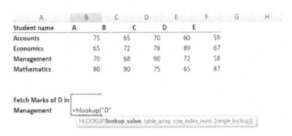

HLOOKUP function in excel has the following arguments:

HLOOKUP (lookup value, table array, row index num, [range lookup])

We must first have the lookup value, as seen in the screenshot above. It will be student D in this case since we need to search his or her Management grades. Now, keep in mind that the lookup value may be a cell relation, a text string, or a numerical value. It will be a student's name in our case, as seen below:

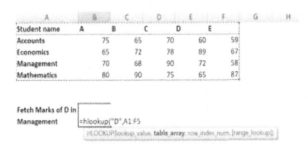

The table array will then be provided as the next move. The lookup value will be checked in a table list, which consists of rows of records. A standard range, a named set, or even an Excel table may create a table array. As a guide, we'll use rows A1 through F5.

Next, we'll describe "row index num," which is the table array cell number from which the value will be retrieved. It will be 4 in this scenario since we are retrieving the value from the fourth row of the specified table.

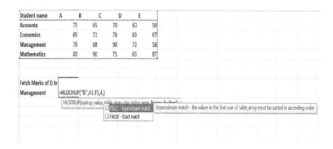

If we were to require marks in Economics, we'd set row index num to 3. Range_lookup is the following command. It causes HLOOKUP to look for a value that is either exact or estimated. That will be False since we are asking for an exact value.

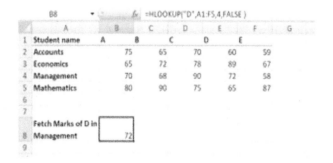

The result will be 72.

9.6 Tips for HLOOKUP Function

- The lookup is case-insensitive. e.g., it would treat the words "TIM" and "Tim" as interchangeable.

- When using HLOOKUP, the "Lookup value" should be the topmost row of the "table array." We'll need to use another Excel calculation if we need to look anywhere else.

- The wildcard characters "*" or "?" are supported by HLOOKUP in the "lookup value" argument (only if the "lookup value" is text).

    Let's look at a case to further grasp this. Assume we are given the following student names and grades:

Student name	Amy	Brain	Cathy	Donald	Ela
Accounts	75	65	70	60	59
Economics	65	72	78	89	67
Management	70	68	90	72	58
Mathematics	80	90	75	65	87

    If we need to use the Horizontal Lookup formula to locate a student's Math marks whose name begins with a "D," the formula is:

    The wild character "*" is used.

- Mistake #N/A—If "range_lookup" is FALSE and the HLOOKUP function cannot locate the "lookup value" in the specified target, it will be returned by HLOOKUP. We may use a function like =IFERROR and insert (HLOOKUP (A4, A1:I2, 2, FALSE), "No meaning found") feature in IFERROR and show our message.

- HLOOKUP will return a #VALUE error if the "row index num" was less than one. Suppose the no. of columns in the table array is greater than the number of rows in the row index num, a #REF error will occur.

- Keep in mind that Excel's HLOOKUP feature will only return one value. This is the first value n that corresponds to the lookup value. What if the table contains a few similar records? In any case, It's best to either delete them or group them in a Pivot table. After that, the array formula can be applied to the Pivot table to retrieve all duplicate values found in the lookup set.

Chapter 10: MS Excel: the TRANSPOSE Function (WS)

The TRANSPOSE function belongs to the Excel Lookup and Reference functions category. A provided set or sequence would be flipped in the opposite direction. A horizontal range can be converted to a vertical array and vice versa using this feature. The TRANSPOSE function is useful in financial analysis for organizing data in the desired format.

The TRANSPOSE feature in Microsoft Excel provides a transposed range of cells. If a vertical spectrum is entered as a parameter, a horizontal array of cells is returned. If a horizontal array of cells is inserted as a parameter, a vertical array of cells is returned.

The TRANSPOSE feature is a Lookup/Reference Function that comes with Excel. It can be found in Excel as a worksheet feature (WS). The TRANSPOSE method is a worksheet function that can be used in a formula in a worksheet cell.

The formula is:

= TRANSPOSE (array)

A range of cells is passed in as the array point. The first row of an array is seen as the first column of the current array, the second row as the second column of the new array, etc.

First, to enter the array formula in Excel, highlight the number of cells where the feature result would be displayed; then type the function in the first cell of the

range and click CTRL-SHIFT-Enter.

10.1 How to use the TRANSPOSE Function in Excel?

In Excel, the TRANSPOSE feature is a built-in tool that can be used as a worksheet function. Find the following scenario to better explain how to utilize TRANSPOSE:

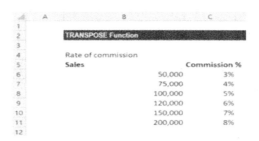

We will use the following formula to transpose the data:

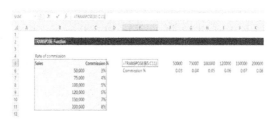

To enter the formula, follow the given steps:

1. First, we'll select any empty cells. They must have the same number of cells as the initial group, but they must be arranged oppositely. e.g., there are eight vertically ordered cells here. As a result, we could choose eight horizontal cells as seen below:

2. The second step is to type **=TRANSPOSE**, as given below:

3. Next, we'll reach the set of cells we'd like to transpose. We need to transpose cells from A2 to B8 in this case. Finally, we'll click CTRL+SHIFT+ENTER.

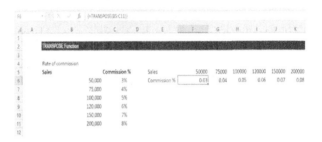

4. When an array is transposed, the first row becomes the current array's first column, and the second row becomes the new array's second column, and so on. As previously said, we must use Control + Shift + Enter to enter the TRANSPOSE feature as an array formula with the same number of cells as the array.

5. The current array must have the same number of rows as the source array has columns, and the new array must have the same number of columns as the source array.

6. We may use Paste Special > TRANSPOSE for yet another conversion.

10.1.1 Dynamic Array vs. Traditional Array

The formulas above were entered in Excel 365, which embraces dynamic array formulas, so there is no need for special syntax, TRANSPOSE functions, and the effects spill into destination cells automatically. TRANSPOSE must be inserted as a multi-cell range formula with control + shift + enter in other variants of Excel:

118

1. Start by choosing a goal range with the same number of rows as the source range's columns and columns as the source range's rows.
2. Pick the source set as the array statement in the TRANSPOSE function.
3. Use control + shift + enter to confirm that the formula is an array formula.

10.2 Tips for the TRANSPOSE Function

- It is not necessary to type the scale by hand. After typing the =TRANSPOSE you can pick the set with your cursor. Simply click and drag from the start to the end of the range. When you're done, note to click CTRL +SHIFT +Enter, not just In.
- Do you need the document and formatting of the cell to be shifted as well? Copy, paste, and then use the Transpose option. However, bear in mind that this will result in duplicates. As a result, if the contents of the original cells shift, the copies will not be changed.
- There's also a lot to discover about array formulas. Create an array algorithm, or learn more about them here, which includes extensive instructions and illustrations.
- A vertical set of cells is returned as a horizontal range by the TRANSPOSE operation or vice versa. The TRANSPOSE method must be entered as an array formula in a sequence of the same number of rows and columns as the resource range's columns and rows, respectively. To change the horizontal and vertical orientation of an array or collection on a worksheet, use TRANSPOSE.

10.3 MS Excel: The COUNTBLANK Function

The COUNTBLANK function is classified as a STATISTICAL function in Excel. COUNTBLANK is a function that counts the number of empty cells in a set of cells. The feature may be helpful in financial analysis for underlining or counting empty cells in a defined set.

The COUNTBLANK feature in Microsoft Excel counts the number of empty cells in a range. The COUNTBLANK function is an Excel built-in function that is classified as a Statistical Function. It can be found in Excel as a worksheet function (WS). The COUNTBLANK function is a worksheet function that can be used in a formula in a worksheet cell.

The formula is:

= COUNTBLANK (range)

Where:

- Range determines the cell range in which blank cells can be counted.
- This function does not count any cells that contain text, numbers, errors, or other data.
- Formulas that return an empty text (") would be counted as blank. Therefore, the COUNTBLANK function counts a cell as blank, including an empty text string or a formula that returns an empty text string.
- Null cells will not be counted if they have a zero.

10.4 How to Use the COUNTBLANK Function in Excel?

This Excel tutorial includes syntax and illustrations for using the COUNTBLANK function. COUNTBLANK is a worksheet feature that can be included in a formula in a worksheet cell. Please find the following scenario to better explain the function's applications: we can find out how many cells are empty using conditional formatting through this function. Let's say we're provided the following information:

We will use this formula = COUNTBLANK (B5:E8) to count the empty rows:

We obtain the following results:

Using the COUNTBLANK function, we may use conditional formatting to emphasize rows of empty cells. Choose the desired range, conditional formatting, and the COUNTBLANK () feature on the conditional formatting tab. This would then show any of the cells in the target range that are blank.

Chapter 11: Convert Numbers into Words

Excel doesn't come with a built-in feature for displaying numbers as English words in a worksheet, but you can integrate it with the Spell Number function code pasted into a VBA (Visual Basic for Applications) module. This feature uses a calculation to translate dollar and cent numbers to terms, so 22.50 will be written as Twenty-two Dollars and Fifty Cents. Instead, use the TEXT feature to translate numeric values to text format without showing them as words.

11.1 How to Convert the Number into Words?

This tutorial of Excel will show you how to transform numbers into words. How can you translate a numerical meaning into words in Microsoft Excel? Might the cell instead display the term "1" for the meaning of one, for example?

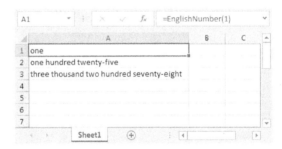

Excel does not have a built-in feature to translate a number to terms. Instead, you'll have to write your custom feature to translate the number into words. Let's have a look at how.

Excel generates macro code while you make a custom function. When you open your spreadsheet after making the custom function, it will alert you that it contains macros. For the feature to operate correctly, you must first allow macros.

Let's get this party underway. First, open your Excel spreadsheet and then click Alt+F11 to bring up the Microsoft Basic Visual for Applications window. Choose Module from the Insert menu.

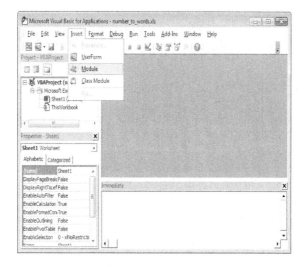

This will create a new Module1 module in your spreadsheet. Copy and paste the two functions below into the innovative module.

Example created by techonthenet.com

Function EnglishNumber (ByVal N as Currency) As String

Const Thousand = 1000@

Const Million = Thousand * Thousand

Const Billion = Thousand * Million

Const Trillion = Thousand * Billion

If (N = 0@) Then EnglishNumber = "zero": Exit Function

```
Dim Buf As String: If (N < 0@) Then Buf = "negative" Else Buf = ""

Dim Frac As Currency: Frac = Abs (N - Fix(N))

If (N < 0@ Or Frac <> 0@) Then N = Abs (Fix(N))

Dim AtLeastOne As Integer: AtLeastOne = N >= 1


If (N >= Trillion) Then

Buf = Buf & EnglishNumberDigitGroup (Int (N / Trillion)) & "trillion"

N = N - Int (N / Trillion) * Trillion

If (N >= 1@) Then Buf = Buf & " "

End If


If (N >= Billion) Then

Buf = Buf & EnglishNumberDigitGroup (Int (N / Billion)) & " billion"

N = N - Int (N / Billion) * Billion

If (N >= 1@) Then Buf = Buf & " "

End If


If (N >= Million) Then

Buf = Buf & EnglishNumberDigitGroup (N \ Million) & " million"

N = N Mod Million
```

If (N >= 1@) Then Buf = Buf & " "

End If

If (N >= Thousand) Then

Buf = Buf & EnglishNumberDigitGroup (N \ Thousand) & " thousand"

N = N Mod Thousand

If (N >= 1@) Then Buf = Buf & " "

End If

If (N >= 1@) Then

Buf = Buf & EnglishNumberDigitGroup(N)

End If

EnglishNumber = Buf

End Function

Private Function EnglishNumberDigitGroup (ByVal N as Integer) As String

Const Hundred = "hundred"

Const One = "one"

```
Const Two = "two"

Const Three = "three"

Const Four = "four"

Const Five = "five"

Const Six = "six"

Const Seven = "seven"

Const Eight = "eight"

Const Nine = "nine"

Dim Buf As String: Buf = ""

Dim Flag as Integer: Flag = False


Select Case (N \ 100)

Case 0: Buf = "": Flag = False

Case 1: Buf = One & Hundred: Flag = True

Case 2: Buf = Two & Hundred: Flag = True

Case 3: Buf = Three & Hundred: Flag = True

Case 4: Buf = Four & Hundred: Flag = True

Case 5: Buf = Five & Hundred: Flag = True

Case 6: Buf = Six & Hundred: Flag = True

Case 7: Buf = Seven & Hundred: Flag = True

Case 8: Buf = Eight & Hundred: Flag = True
```

```
Case 9: Buf = Nine & Hundred: Flag = True

End Select


If (Flag <> False) Then N = N Mod 100

If (N > 0) Then

If (Flag <> False) Then Buf = Buf & " "

Else

EnglishNumberDigitGroup = Buf

Exit Function

End If


Select Case (N \ 10)

Case 0, 1: Flag = False

Case 2: Buf = Buf & "twenty": Flag = True

Case 3: Buf = Buf & "thirty": Flag = True

Case 4: Buf = Buf & "forty": Flag = True

Case 5: Buf = Buf & "fifty": Flag = True

Case 6: Buf = Buf & "sixty": Flag = True

Case 7: Buf = Buf & "seventy": Flag = True

Case 8: Buf = Buf & "eighty": Flag = True

Case 9: Buf = Buf & "ninety": Flag = True
```

```
End Select


If (Flag <> False) Then N = N Mod 10

If (N > 0) Then

If (Flag <> False) Then Buf = Buf & "-"

Else

EnglishNumberDigitGroup = Buf

Exit Function

End If


Select Case (N)

Case 0:

Case 1: Buf = Buf & One

Case 2: Buf = Buf & Two

Case 3: Buf = Buf & Three

Case 4: Buf = Buf & Four

Case 5: Buf = Buf & Five

Case 6: Buf = Buf & Six

Case 7: Buf = Buf & Seven

Case 8: Buf = Buf & Eight

Case 9: Buf = Buf & Nine
```

```
Case 10: Buf = Buf & "ten"

Case 11: Buf = Buf & "eleven"

Case 12: Buf = Buf & "twelve"

Case 13: Buf = Buf & "thirteen"

Case 14: Buf = Buf & "fourteen"

Case 15: Buf = Buf & "fifteen"

Case 16: Buf = Buf & "sixteen"

Case 17: Buf = Buf & "seventeen"

Case 18: Buf = Buf & "eighteen"

Case 19: Buf = Buf & "nineteen"

End Select


EnglishNumberDigitGroup = Buf


End Function
```

Your Excel window should be as given below:

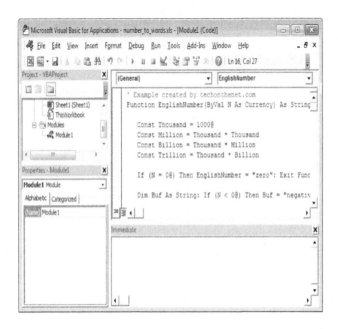

Return to your spreadsheet window and click the Save button (disk icon). You can now translate a number to words with the EnglishNumber function. It will behave in the same way as any other worksheet function. Simply type the following into your Excel spreadsheet to use the EnglishNumber function:

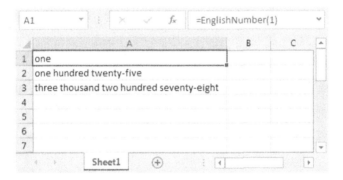

The EnglishNumber feature will return the following based on the spreadsheet above:

=EnglishNumber (1)

RESULT: "one"

=EnglishNumber (125)

RESULT: "one hundred twenty-five."

=EnglishNumber (3278)

RESULT: "three thousand two hundred seventy-eight."

Chapter 12: Excel Data Entry Form

Excel has a specific method for entering data into a spreadsheet that allows the process quicker, more user-friendly, and less error-prone, particularly in large worksheets of dozens or even hundreds of columns.

How do people usually fill out Excel tables? Through simply typing data into cells. You will need to scroll up to see the column headings or right to see the column headings before returning to the table's beginning. When working with vast data sets, It's easy to get things mixed up and insert data in the wrong cell.

You may ask Excel to show one row of details in a convenient dialog box to make feedback easier. You may add new documents, as well as update and delete old ones, in this section. Data Validation may also be set up to guarantee that only submissions that follow those conditions are accepted.

The Data Entry Form in Excel functions as follows:

Why do you should know about data entry forms?

When it comes to data entry in Excel, there are two general problems you've encountered (and seen others encounter):

1. It takes a long time. You must first insert the data in one cell, then move on to the next cell and repeat the process. You will need to scroll up to see which column you're in and what details you need to join. If there are more columns, scroll to the right and then back to the top.
2. It is prone to errors. If you have an extensive data collection that requires 40 entries, there's a chance you'll join anything that wasn't meant for that cell.

A data entry type may assist by rendering the operation more efficient and error-free.

An organization's recruiting staff usually maintains the data collection below.

When a person must add a new record, he or she must first pick a cell in the next empty row, then render the entry for each column cell by cell. While this is an entirely acceptable method, a Data Entry Form in Excel will be more effective. You may enter data into this data collection using the data entry method below.

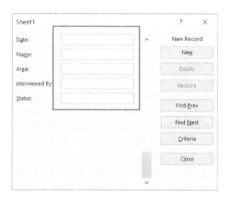

The details will be entered in the highlighted areas. When you're done, press Enter to render the data element of the table and pass it on to the next entry.

If you will see, this is more convenient than traditional data entry since it is included in a single dialog box.

Using an Excel data entry method generally requires any pre-work.

You'll find that Excel doesn't have a data entry type option (not in any tab in the ribbon).

- You must first connect it to a Quick Access Toolbar before you can use it.

12.1 Parts of the Data Entry Form

There are several buttons on an Excel Data Entry Form. Here's a brief overview of what each button is for:

- **New:** This clears all old data in the form and lets you generate a new one.
- **Delete:** You can use this to get rid of an existing record. If you press the Delete key in the above case, the record for Mike Banes would be deleted.
- **Restore:** You can restore the previous data in the form (if you haven't pressed New or hit Enter) if you're updating a current entry.
- **Find previous:** This will locate the preceding entry.
- **Find next:** This will locate the following page.

- **Criteria:** Using criteria, you may locate unique documents. e.g., if you want to search all the records that the applicant was hired, you must first press a Criteria button, then enter "Hired" in the Status field before using the find buttons.
- **Close:** This will bring the form to a close.
- **The scroll bar:** Can be used to navigate through the documents.

Let's have a look at what you can do in an Excel Data Entry form. To open a dialog box for the Data Entry form, you must first translate the data into an Excel Table and then choose every cell in the table. If you don't choose the cell in an Excel Table, you'll get a prompt like this:

12.2 Creating Another New Entry

The measures to make a new entry in Excel using the Data Entry Form are as follows:

1. In the Excel Table, choose any cell.

2. In the Quick Access Toolbar, choose the Form button.

3. Fill in the form fields with your details.

4. Press Enter (or select the New button) to add the record to the table and provide a blank form for the next document.

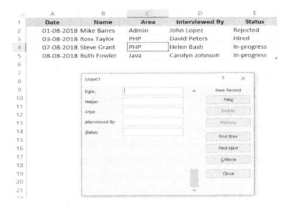

12.3 Adding Data Entry Form Option

The steps for adding the data entry type alternative to the Quick Access Toolbar are as follows:

1. Right-click on each of the Quick Access Toolbar's current icons. Select "Customize Quick Access Toolbar" from the drop-down menu.

2. Choose the "All Commands" choice from the drop-down menu in the "Excel Options" dialog box that appears.

3. Select "Form" from the list of commands at the bottom of the page.

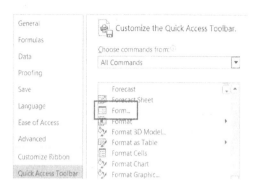

4. Press on the add button.

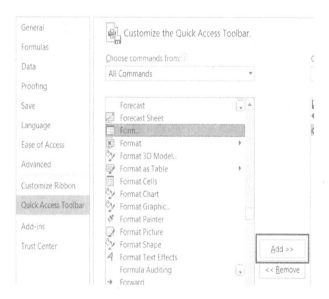

5. Click on OK.

These steps would add the Form icon to the Quick Access Toolbar (as given below).

12.4 Navigating Through the Existing Records

One of the advantages of utilizing Form for Data Entry is browsing and updating the documents without dropping the dialog box. This is particularly helpful if your dataset has a lot of columns. This would save you a lot of time scrolling and moving back and forth.

The measures for navigating and editing documents using a data entry method are as follows:

1. In the Excel Table, choose any cell.
2. In the Quick Access Toolbar, choose the Form button.
3. Click the "Find Next" button to move to the next page and the "Find Prev" button to enter the last entry.

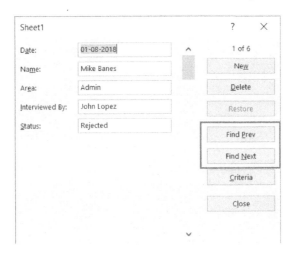

4. To adjust an entry, type it in and press enter. Click the "Restore" button if you want to go back to the initial entry (and you haven't reached the enter key yet).
5. You may also use the scroll bar to go from one entry to the next.

If you want to run through all the entries with the status "In-progress," follow these steps:

In the Excel row, choose any cell.

In the Quick Access Toolbar, choose the Form button.

Click a Criteria button in the Data Entry Form dialog window.

Enter "In-progress" in the status field.

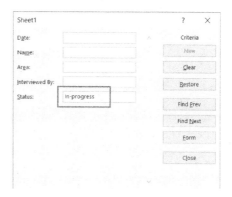

1. Go through the Find Prev/Find Next buttons to navigate the entries where the status is still in In-progress.
2. When you have a large dataset and want to quickly go through the documents that follow a collection of standards, Criteria is a helpful function.
3. To navigate through the results, keep in mind that you may use several parameter fields.
4. E.g., if you want to look at all the "In-progress" records created with 07-08-2018, you can use the parameters ">07-08-2018" in the "Date" field and "In-progress" as the status field value. When you use the Find Next/Find Prev buttons to search, it will now only display records created with 07-08-2018 with the state In-progress.

Whether you entered the data inconsistently and using variants of a phrase (such as In-progress, in progress, and InProgress), you'll need to use wildcard characters to find certain documents. The measures to do so are as follows:

In the Excel row, choose any cell.

In the Quick Access Toolbar, choose the Form icon.

Choose Criteria from the drop-down menu.

Enter "progress" in the status field.

12.5 Deleting a Record

The Data Entry form itself allows you to erase information. This is handy when you try to search and uninstall a certain form of document. The measures to erase a record using Data Entry Form are as follows:

1. In the Excel row, choose any cell.
2. In the Quick Access Toolbar, choose the Form icon.
3. Find the record you intend to erase and delete it.
4. To delete something, press the Delete key.

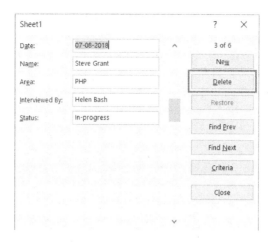

12.6 How to Make a Data Entry Form in Excel?

Only a properly operational Excel table will include a data entry type. To get the request, simply enter your information in a table and press the Form icon. The following are the detailed steps:

1. Type the headings of the column in the topmost row of the worksheet as usual. Skip this move if you need an input type for a current data collection.
2. Choose every cell in your dataset and press Ctrl + T at the same time. This will pick all the information and transform it into a chart.
3. Press the Form button with your mouse anywhere on the table. It's over.

Let's use this little table as an example to keep it simple:

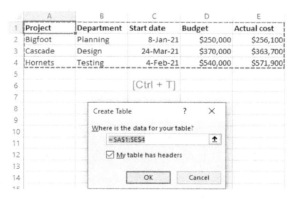

When you click the Form icon, a data entry form for your table appears, with fields referring to the column headings:

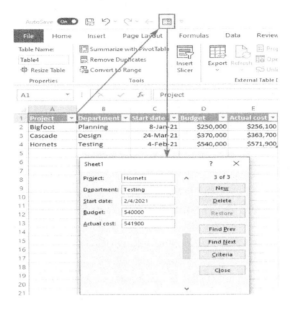

The Excel input type, as you can see, has a variety of keys. Here's a quick rundown of each button's function:

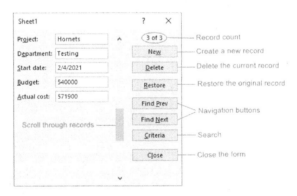

Besides these buttons, you can use the following ones for navigation:

- Tab—get to the next field.
- Shift + Tab—get to the previous field.
- Enter—save the current record and start a new one.

12.6.1 How to Add a New Record?

Follow these measures to introduce a new record to the table using the data entry form:

1. Go to every cell on your table and choose it.
2. On the Quick Access Toolbar or the ribbon, click the Form button.
3. Press the New button in the input form.
4. Fill in the blanks with the necessary detail.
5. When you're done, press Enter or touch the New button once more. The record will be added to the table, and a blank form will be created for the next record.

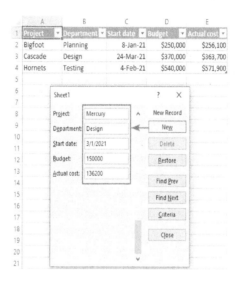

Press Ctrl +; to insert **today's date**.

Press Ctrl + Shift +; to enter the **current time**.

12.6.2 How to Quest for Records?

1. Find Next keys and the Find Prev keys, and the vertical roll bar can be used to go through all the records one by one. Using a Criteria button to search records that follow specific criteria.

2. To find all the assignments allocated to the Design department, for example, style Design in the Department area and click on the Find Next:

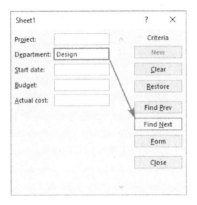

You may use wildcard characters to extend the search. For example, type *skill* in the Project area to find projects with the word "skill" somewhere in the name.

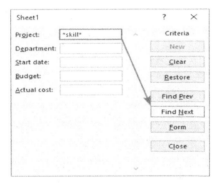

The logical operators are greater than (>), less than (), equivalent to (=), not equal to (>), and others come in handy when coping with numbers and dates. E.g., to see documents with a start date before 1-Mar-2021, use the criterion "1-Mar-2021" or "3/1/2021":

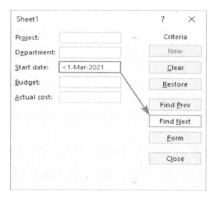

12.6.3 How to Update and Restore Records?

1. You may use the Criteria or navigation buttons to get to a record, change the incorrect sector, and press Enter to commit the modified data to the table if an entry is obsolete or contains incorrect records.

2. If you accidentally changed everything but didn't press Enter yet, you can restore the original record by pressing the Restore icon. If you've already pressed Enter and the updates have been applied to the table, click Ctrl + Z to undo the process.

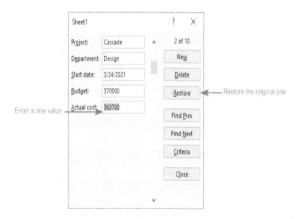

12.7 How to Use the Data Validation Along With the Data Entry Form?

Establish a data validity rule for one or more columns in your table to limit user feedback to a specific data class, and the guidelines will be carried over to the data entry form automatically.

To restrict the Budget to numbers within a certain range, for example, we establish the following rule:

An error warning (either the normal or your custom one) will appear if anyone attempts to submit a value that does not comply with the rule you've set:

12.7.1 Limitation: Drop Lists Are Unavailable For a Form

One drawback of using data validation for input forms is that drop-down lists do not exist in data entry fields. And if a drop-down list isn't visible within the form, the limitations it imposes in place. If you enter a value on the chart, the form will refuse it automatically for Data Validation.

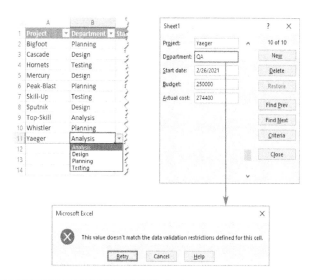

12.8 Formulas in Data Entry Forms

If one or more columns in your table are determined using calculations, you won't be able to change them using the form since the calculation result is shown as text rather than an editable area. While this might seem to be just another restriction, it serves a purpose. When you adjust a table formula in one cell, it immediately changes the formulas in all other cells in the same column. Formula editing on the input form is disabled to prevent data corruption.

e.g., depending on the 5% level, you could use the following calculation to determine if the real cost is under, above, or above the budget:

=IF (ABS ([@ [Actual cost]]/ [@Budget] - 1) <=5%, "Within budget," IF ([@ [Actual cost]]/ [@Budget]- 1>5%, "Over budget," IF ([@ [Actual cost]]/ [@Budget]- 1<5%, "Under budget," "")))

If you have a Microsoft 365 subscription and have signed up for the Beta Channel (Office Insider), you can use the LET feature to wrap the above formula as seen below. This will render the method more efficient, understandable, and measure faster:

=LET (dif, E2/D2-1, IF (ABS (dif)<=5%, "Within budget," IF (dif>5%, "Over budget," IF (dif<5%, "Under budget," ""))))

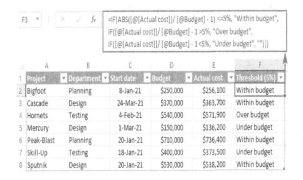

You can only see a non-editable estimated outcome on the data entry type, not the formula:

12.9 How to Open the Data Entry Form With VBA?

Your users might not be aware of where to search for the Form button while you're setting up a table for anyone else. Furthermore, they might be unaware that such a thing happens. You may use a macro to bring the input type into view. Place a single key directly in the worksheet to execute the macro.

If the current sheet contains a table, you only need one line of code to open the form:

```
Sub OpenDataEntryForm ()

ActiveSheet.ShowDataForm

End Sub
```

However, there is one important caveat: the coding mentioned above would only function if one of the following conditions is met:

Your table starts in A1; or

Your table has the name "Database" (a given name, not a table name).

To get around these restrictions, use the advanced version of the code, which defines the cell where your table starts (in our case, B2), names the current area "database," opens the form, and then deletes the name:

```
Sub OpenDataEntryForm ()

Dim nName as Name

Range("B2"). CurrentRegion.Name = "database"

ActiveSheet.ShowDataForm

For Each nName In ActiveWorkbook.Names

If "database" = nName.Name, then nName.Delete

Next nName

End Sub
```

You should then add a button type control to your worksheet and allocate a macro to it after adding the file. Alternatively, you may make a button out of a form or some object.

Users will now easily access the input data type by pressing a brightly colored mouse. They don't even need to worry about placing the cursor inside the table; the form will open regardless of which cell is currently working.

Chapter 13: Excel Valuation Modeling

Discounted Cash Flow (DCF) Analysis, relative trade multiples, precedent trades, and vertical and horizontal analysis ratios are only a few examples of valuation modeling in Excel. The different forms of analyses may either be created from scratch in Excel or based on a current framework or model. A diverse variety of finance practitioners do this style of job regularly.

13.1 Why Perform Valuation Modeling in Excel?

Valuation modeling in Excel is helpful for various purposes, and people from a variety of sectors devote a considerable amount of time using it. The following are some of the reasons:

151

- Being ready to collect money from investors.
- Selling a business and determining what price point to consider.
- Buying a business and determining how much to offer for it.
- Issuing stock to workers (an Employee Share Ownership Plan or ESOP).
- Internal budgeting and preparation.
- Market succession planning.
- Procurement prospects and capital programs evaluation.
- Impairment testing (for every substantial decrease in asset values)
- Legal action, such as insolvency.

13.2 How to Execute Excel Valuation Modeling?

Valuation modeling in excel has different types of modeling like:

13.2.1 Discounted Cash Flow Modeling in Excel

A finance specialist uses the DCF methodology to bring 3–5 years of past financial data for a company into an Excel model. They then join the three financial statements together to provide a complex connection.

Based on predictions of how the company will work in the future, Excel calculations are used to construct a prediction for the future. Finally, they measure the business's terminal value and use its weighted average cost of capital to discount the projection timeframe and terminal value down to the current.

FINANCIAL STATEMENTS			2013	2014	Historical Results 2015	2016	2017	2018	Forecast Period 2019	2020	2021	2022
Balance Sheet Check			OK	OK	OK	OK	OK	OK	OK	OK	OK	OK

DCF Model

Assumptions
Tax Rate	25%
Discount Rate	12%
Perpetual Growth Rate	4%
EV/EBITDA Multiple	8.0x
Transaction Date	3/31/2018
Fiscal Year End	12/31/2018
Current Price	16.00
Shares Outstanding	20,000

Discounted Cash Flow	Entry	2018	2019	2020	2021	2022	Exit	Terminal Value	
Date	2018-03-31	2018-12-31	2019-12-31	2020-12-31	2021-12-31	2022-12-31	2022-12-31	EV/EBITDA	812,428
Time Periods		0	1	2	3	4			
Year Fraction		0.75	1.00	1.00	1.00	1.00			
EBIT		39,866	36,890	37,013	74,263	86,887			
Less: Cash Taxes		9,966	9,223	9,253	18,566	21,722			
NOPAT		29,899	27,668	27,759	55,697	65,165			
Plus: D&A		13,132	13,786	14,211	14,487	14,667			
EBITDA		52,998	50,676	51,224	88,750	101,554			
Less: Capex		15,000	15,000	15,000	15,000	15,000			
Less: Changes in NWC		3,175	5,062	5,768	(2,613)	2,041			
Unlevered FCF		24,856	21,391	21,203	57,797	62,791	812,428		
Transaction FCFF	-	18,642	21,391	21,203	57,797	62,791	812,428		
IRR FCFF	(210,450)	18,642	21,391	21,203	57,797	62,791	812,428		

Intrinsic Value		Market Value		Rate of Return	
Enterprise Value	598,465	Market Cap	320,000	Current Price	16.00
Plus: Cash	139,550	Plus: Debt	30,000	Target Price	35.40
Less: Debt	30,000	Less: Cash	139,550	Target Price Upside	121%
Equity Value	708,015	Enterprise Value	210,450	IRR	43%
Equity Value/Share	35.40	Equity Value/Share	16.00		

13.2.2 Equivalent Trading Multiples in Excel

The methodology to equivalent multiples valuation modeling in Excel differs significantly from that of the DCF model. Instead of assessing a company's inherent value, an investor would examine the valuation multiples of other publicly listed firms and correlate them to the valuation multiples of the business(es) in question. EV/Revenue, EV/EBITDA, EV/EBIT, Price/Earnings, and Price/Book are several instances of valuation multiples.

Company Name	Market Data				Financial Data (FY+1)			Valuation (FY+1)		
	Price ($/share)	Shares (M)	Market Cap ($M)	Net Debt	EV ($M)	Sales ($M)	EBITDA ($M)	Earnings ($M)	EV/Sales x	EV/EBITDA x	P/E x
Micro Partners	$9.45	100	$945	$125	$1,070	$268	$76	$47	4.0x	14.1x	20.1x
Junior Enterprises	$5.68	1,250	$7,100	$2,000	$9,100	$4,136	$778	$412	2.2x	11.7x	17.2x
Minature Company	$18.11	50	$906	$25	$931	$443	$96	$56	2.1x	9.7x	16.3x
Average Limited	$12.27	630	$7,730	$350	$8,080	$1,949	$528	$294	4.1x	15.3x	26.3x
Behemoth Industries	$9.03	1,500	$13,545	$0	$13,545	$6,622	$795	$423	2.0x	17.0x	32.0x
Average									2.9x	13.6x	22.4x
Median									2.2x	14.1x	20.1x

13.2.3 Precedent Transaction Modeling in Excel

An investor can use the third method of Excel value simulation to look at the rates charged for previous mergers and acquisitions (M&A) in related companies. This is often a type of relative valuation, although, unlike similar trading multiples, these deals contain acquisition premiums (control value) and are focused on historical data (which can quickly become out of date).

Date	Target	Transaction Value ($M)	Buyers	Financial Data			Valuation		
				Sales	EBITDA	EBIT	EV/Sales	EV/EBITDA	EV/EBIT
01-24-2018	Current Ltd	2,350	Average Limited	1,237			1.9x	na	na
04-19-2016	Recent Inc	6,500	Behemoth Industries	4,643	808	515	1.4x	8.0x	12.6x
04-19-2014	Past Co	2,150	Other Group	1,993	249	178	1.3x	8.7x	12.1x
11-07-2014	Historical LLP	450	Junior Enterprises	197			2.3x	na	na
11-01-2012	Old Group	325	Minature Company	64	17	15	5.1x	18.8x	21.5x
10-07-2011	Dated Enterprises	150	Micro Partners	71	16		2.1x	9.3x	na
Average							2.3x	11.2x	15.4x
Median							2.0x	9.0x	12.6x

The significant skills required for valuation modeling are:

- Accountancy (principles, financial statements, methods.
- Finance (financial math, ratios, formulas, calculations.
- Microsoft Excel (MS Excel shortcuts, best practices, functions).
- Strategic plan (market analysis, competitive advantage).
- Valuation (a mixture of all the preceding skills).

13.3 Jobs That Perform Valuation Modeling in Excel

Many occupations and career options require the ability to value a brand, a business segment, or a potential investment opportunity in Excel. The following are some of the more popular jobs that need those abilities:

- Betting on investments (analyst and associate level).
- Venture capital and private equity (analyst and associate level).
- Business growth (analyst and manager level).
- Budgeting and financial reporting (analyst, manager, and director level).
- Accounting in the public sector (transaction advisory, impairment testing).
- Study on the stock market (associate and analyst level).

13.4 Main Valuation Methods

Industry experts employ three critical assessment approaches when valuing a business as a going concern: (1) DCF research, (2) equivalent company analysis, and (3) precedent transactions. In investment management, private equity, market analysis, business growth, Leveraged Buyouts (LBO), Mergers & Acquisitions (M&A), and several other fields of finance, these are the most traditional types of valuation.

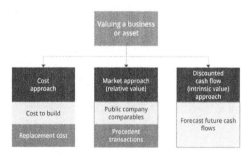

13.4.1 Comparable Analysis ("Comps")

The Comparable Company Analysis (also known as "trading multiples," "peer association analysis," or "public sector multiples" or "equity comps,") is a comparative valuation approach in which you look at trading multiples just like EV/EBITDA, P/E, or other measures that equate the actual value of a company to that of other related companies. The most popular way of valuation is using multiples of EBITDA.

The "comps" valuation approach establishes a measurable value for the company dependent on the existing market value of similar businesses. Comps are the most used method since they are simple to quantify and still up to date. According to the rationale, if a company X trades at 10-times P/E ratio & company Y earns $2.50 per share, company Y's stock would be worth $25.00 a share, according to the rationale (assuming the companies have similar attributes).

	Market Data			Financial Data (FY+1)			Valuation (FY+1)		
Company Name	Price ($/share)	Market Cap ($M)	EV ($M)	Sales ($M)	EBITDA ($M)	Earnings ($M)	EV/Sales x	EV/EBITDA x	P/E x
Micro Partners	$9.45	$945	$1,070	$268	$76	$47	2.5x	14.1x	22.8x
Junior Enterprises	$5.68	$7,100	$9,100	$4,136	$778	$412	2.2x	11.7x	22.1x
Minature Company	$18.11	$906	$931	$443	$96	$56	1.9x	9.7x	16.7x
Average Limited	$12.27	$7,730	$8,080	$1,949	$528	$294	2.6x	12.2x	22.4x
Bohemeth Industires	$9.03	$13,545	$13,545	$5,622	$795	$423	1.7x	17.0x	28.3x
Average							2.2x	12.9x	22.5x
Median							2.2x	12.2x	22.4x

13.4.2 Precedent Transactions

Another form of relative assessment is precedent transactions evaluation, which compares the firm in question to other companies in the same market that has previously been sold or purchased. Both sale values comprise the take-over fee that was included in the purchase price.

The numbers reflect a company's total worth. They're helpful for M&A deals, but they may quickly get out of date and no longer represent the current demand as time goes by. Comps or stock trading multiples are most widely used.

	Transaction			Valuation		
Date	Target	Value ($M)	Buyers	EV/Sales	EV/EBITDA	EV/EBIT
01/24/2017	Current Ltd	2,350	Average Limited	1.9x	9.4x	11.2x
04/19/2016	Recent Inc	6,500	Bohemeth Industires	1.4x	8.0x	12.6x
04/19/2014	Past Co	2,150	Other Group	1.3x	8.7x	12.1x
11/07/2014	Historical LLP	450	Junior Enterprises	2.3x	11.1x	13.6x
11/01/2012	Old Group	325	Minature Company	5.1x	18.8x	21.5x
10/07/2011	Dated Enterprises	150	Micro Partners	2.1x	9.3x	13.2x
Average				2.3x	10.9x	14.0x
Median				2.0x	9.4x	12.9x

13.4.3 DCF Analysis

An investor predicts the company's free cash flow in the forthcoming and discounts it back to today at the firm's Weighted Average Cost of Capital in a discounted cash flow (DCF) study (WACC).

A DCF research is carried out by creating a financial model in Excel, and it requires a great deal of information and analysis. It's the most in-depth of the three methods, and it requires the most predictions and conclusions. The time and effort took to prepare a DCF model, on the other hand, also yields the most precise valuation. The analyst will use a DCF model to predict value dependent on various scenarios and do a sensitivity analysis.

For larger companies, the DCF value is typically calculated using a sum-of-the-parts analysis, in which various business divisions are modeled separately and then applied together.

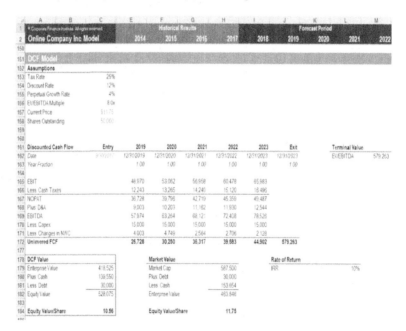

Chapter 14: Mathematical and Statistical Functions

Functions, in comparison to formulas, are another way to do mathematical calculations in Excel. A quantitative method is applied to a set of cells in a worksheet using statistical functions. The SUM function, for example, is used to add the values in a set of cells. The table shows a list of widely employed statistical features. When implementing a mathematical method to a set of cells, functions are more potent than formulas. You'd have to apply each cell position to the calculation one at a time if you used a formula to add the values in several cells. If you must apply the values in a few hundred cell positions, this will take a long time. When you use a function, you will quickly highlight all the cells that hold the values you want to sum.

14.1 Excel Math Functions

Excel provides many simple and advanced features for performing mathematical operations, such as calculating exponentials, logarithms, and factorials. The functions collection itself will require many pages to write. So, let's go through a few simple math functions that you might find helpful in your everyday tasks. The following are four essential Excel functions for adding up the values of cells in each set.

14.1.1 SUM Function

The sum of its arguments is returned by SUM (number1, [number2],). Numbers, cell references, and formula-driven numeric values may both be used as arguments.

For instance, the simplest math formula =SUM(A1:A3,1) adds the values in cells A1, A2, and A3 together, adding 1 to the result.

14.1.2 SUMIF and SUMIFS Functions

Both roles sum up all the cells in a spectrum that satisfy a set of criteria. The distinction is that SUMIF can only assess one criterion, while SUMIFS can evaluate several criteria.

SUMIFS (sum range, criteria range1, criteria1, [criteria range2, criteria2] ...) SUMIF (range, criteria, [sum range])

- Range/criteria range—the range of cells that the corresponding requirements may test.
- Criterion—a requirement that must be satisfied.
- Sum_range—cells that would be added if the condition is true.

The following image illustrates how the SUMIFS and SUMIF functions can be applied to real-world data:

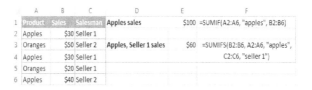

14.1.3 SUMPRODUCT Function

The Function SUMPRODUCT (array1, array2...) is only a few array-handling functions in Microsoft Excel. It multiplies the components of the supplied sequence and returns the total of the results.

14.2 Statistical Functions in Excel

A few Excel statistical functions that anybody may recognize and use for technical data processing among several extremely specialized Excel statistical functions consist of identifying the highest, lowest, and cumulative values.

- **MIN (number1, [number2], ...)**—returns the minimum value from the list of arguments.

- **MAX (number1, [number2], ...)**—returns the maximum value from the list of arguments

- **AVERAGE (number1, [number2], ...)**—returns the average of the arguments.

- **SMALL (array, k)**—returns the K, the smallest value in the array.

- **LARGE (array, k)**—returns the K, the largest value in the array.

The following one explains the basic statistical functions in action.

	A	B	C	D	E
1	Numbers		Min:	1	=MIN(A2:A9)
2		1			
3		9	Max:	10	=MAX(A2:A9)
4		2			
5		5	Average:	5.75	=AVERAGE(A2:A9)
6		7			
7		4	2nd smallest:	2	=SMALL(A2:A9, 2)
8		10			
9		8	3rd largest:	8	=LARGE(A2:A9, 3)

14.2.1 Excel Financial Functions

Accounting administrators, financial analysts, and banking professionals may use Microsoft Excel to make their jobs easier. So far, we've just covered one financial feature in this book, which can be used to measure compound interest.

Financial Function Examples:

FV (rate, nper, pmt, [pv], [type])—calculates the future value of an investment based on a constant interest rate.

14.2.2 Excel Text Functions (String Functions)

To control text strings, Microsoft Excel has a plethora of features. The following are the most important:

TEXT Function

- **TEXT (value, format_text)** is used to convert a number or a date into a text string in the specified format, where:

- **Value** is a numeric value that you want to convert into text.
- **Format_text** is the desired format.
- The resulting formulas explain the TEXT function in Excel in action:

- **=TEXT (A1," mm/dd/yyyy")** - alter a date in cell A1 in a text string in the traditional US date format, such as "01/01/2015" (month/day/year).

- **=TEXT (A1,"€#, ##0.00")** - converts a number in A1 into a currency text string such as "€3.00."

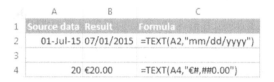

14.2.3 Logical Functions in Excel

Microsoft Excel has several logical functions that calculate and return a value based on a set of conditions.

AND, OR, XOR Functions

- AND (logical1, [logical2], ...)—returns TRUE if all the arguments evaluate TRUE, FALSE otherwise.
- OR (logical1, [logical2]...)—returns TRUE if at least one of the arguments is TRUE.

- XOR (logical1, [logical2]...)—returns a LOGICAL EXCLUSIVE OR of all arguments.

	A	B	C	D	E
1	Number 1	Number 2	AND	OR	XOR
2			=AND(A2=0, B2=0)	=OR(A2=0, B2=0)	=XOR(A2=0, B2=0)
3	1	0	FALSE	TRUE	TRUE
4	1	1	FALSE	FALSE	FALSE
5	0	0	TRUE	TRUE	FALSE

Chapter 15: Use of Five Advanced Excel Pivot Table Techniques

PivotTables are one of the most common financial methods, so anybody who uses Excel should know how to use them. You can easily do data processing for it.

We'll walk you through how to create the first PivotTable in Excel, as well as the advanced features you can use to configure your data and create reports, dashboards, and more in this multi-part tutorial.

Are you prepared to learn how to use PivotTables in Microsoft Excel?

Continue reading the written book for a walkthrough on using each of these five features: Slicers, Timelines, Calculated Fields, Tabular View, and Recommended PivotTables. Let's get started.

15.1 Slicers

Slicers are point-and-click software that enables you to fine-tune the data in your Excel PivotTable. With the aid of a slicer, you can conveniently adjust the data in your PivotTable.

The PivotTable only displays the object in the table after you select Backpack.

You can also create PivotTable reports that many people can see. Adding slicers to your report would enable your end-user to configure it to their taste.

To install a slicer, go to the Analyze tab on Excel's ribbon and press within your PivotTable.

To have a set of columns, check several boxes, each with its slicer.

To multi-select objects inside a slicer, hold Control on your keyboard. This may require several choices from a column as part of your PivotTable data.

15.2 Timelines

Timelines are a kind of slicer that can be used to change the dates in your PivotTable results. If the data contains dates, you can consider using Timelines to pick data from time frames.

To insert a Timeline to your advanced Excel PivotTable, go to Analyze > Insert Timeline. A Timeline is a specific kind of slicer that manages the data in your advanced Excel PivotTable depending on the date.

To add a Timeline, make sure you've chosen a PivotTable (click within it) and then go to Excel's ribbon and choose Insert > Timeline. To build a timeline, check the box of your date column (or several columns) in the pop-up window and click OK.

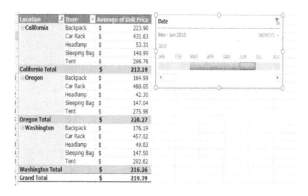

To have a particular time range for the PivotTable, click and drag inside the timeline frame.

You can adjust what's included in the PivotTable by clicking and dragging the handles in the timeline after added.

165

Tap the dropdown box in the lower right corner to adjust the way your Timeline functions. Instead of displaying individual dates on the timeline, you may adjust it to display details by quarter or year, for example.

15.3 Tabular View

Excel's default PivotTable display resembles a waterfall, with more "layers" in the details as you drag more levels of fields into the rows box.

The issue is that calculations are challenging to compose on PivotTables in the traditional view. If you have your data in a Pivot Table but want to use it in a more conventional spreadsheet format, you can use a tabular view.

To function with your PivotTable in a regular spreadsheet format, go to Design > Report Layout > Display in Tabular Form.

Let the PivotTable appear like regular rows and columns display by using the Tabular View.

15.4 Calculated Fields

Calculated fields enable you to add a column to your PivotTable that was not present in the original data. You will generate entirely new fields to deal in by using standard math operations. Take two existing columns and combine them with math to make a whole new one.

Consider the following scenario: we have revenue details in a database. We know how many products were produced and how much each item cost. This is the ideal period to measure the order amount using a calculated field.

Start by clicking within a PivotTable and then clicking Analyze on the ribbon to get started with measured fields. Then choose Calculated Field from the Fields, Items & Sets menu.

To add a calculated field to your PivotTable, go to Analyze > Fields, Items & Sets > Calculated Field.

Begin by giving the measured area a name in the new pop-up window. The amount multiplied by the price of each unit equals the overall order price. Then, in the list of fields in this browser, you'll double-click on the first field name (quantity).

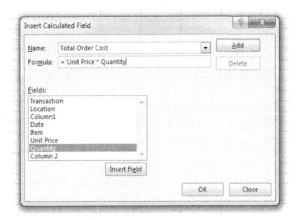

You multiplied the current Unit Price field by the Quantity field to get the overall order rate.

You'll apply the multiplication symbol, *, and then double-click on the complete quantity after you've inserted the field term. Let's move ahead and click the OK button.

Excel has now added the latest measured area to advanced PivotTable. The list of PivotTables would also appear in the list of fields, allowing you to drag and drop it anywhere you need it in the report.

You may type your integer values in the measured area if you don't want to use math on two columns. For instance, if you just wanted to apply 5% sales tax to each order, you might enter the following estimated field:

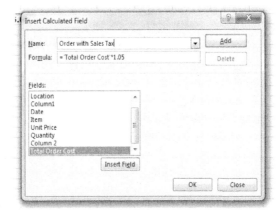

To measure a cost like sales tax, multiplied the overall order cost by 1.05; you can use integer values in addition to existing fields.

Calculated fields will include all regular math operators, including addition, subtraction, multiplication, and division. When you don't want to refresh the original results, use these calculated areas.

15.5 Recommended Pivot Tables

It feels like cheating to use the Recommended PivotTables feature. You notice yourself beginning with one of the recommended setups rather than dragging and lowering areas.

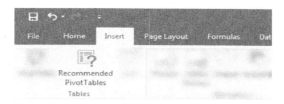

Go to Insert > Recommended PivotTables.

There isn't anything to talk about this function since it is too easy to use. You will use it to quickly build specialized Pivot Tables in Excel. Select your results, then go to the Insert tab on the Excel ribbon and select Recommended PivotTables.

A plethora of choices for generating a PivotTable from your original data is available in the pop-up window. To see the Recommended PivotTable options Excel created, click through the thumbnails on the left side of the window.

The suggested PivotTable functionality provides several one-click solutions for data analysis.

Even if this is a more sophisticated feature that few users consider, It's a perfect way to get started with PivotTables. Nothing keeps you from manipulating the fields on your own to change the PivotTable, so this is a time-saving starting point.

Chapter 16: Create Charts in Excel: Types and Examples

A chart is a representation of data in both columns and rows in a graphic format. Charts are commonly used to analyze data sets for trends and patterns. Assume you've been keeping track of revenue data in Excel for the last three years. You will see which year had the most revenue and which year had the least when looking at charts. You may also use charts to equate defined goals to actual accomplishments.

16.1 Types of Charts

Excel has a variety of chart formats that you can use to do this. The form of chart you choose is determined by the data you want to represent. Excel 2013 and later have a feature that analyzes the data and recommends the chart form you can use, making it easier for users.

The table below lists some of the most widely used charts and what they can be used.

S/N	CHART TYPE	WHEN SHOULD I USE IT?	EXAMPLE
1	Pie Chart	When you want to quantify items and show them as percentages.	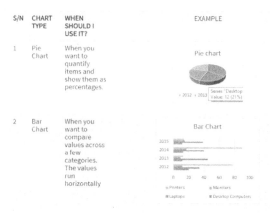
2	Bar Chart	When you want to compare values across a few categories. The values run horizontally	

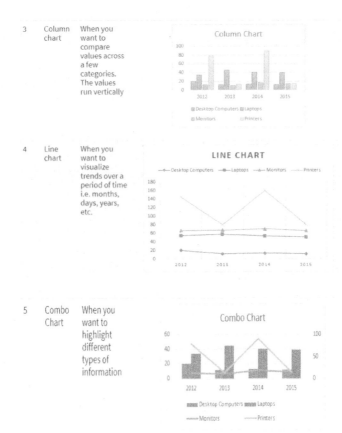

16.1.1 Importance of Charts

- Helps to visualize data graphically.
- Makes it easy to analyze trends and patterns in charts.
- Data in cells is more difficult to understand.

16.2 Step by Step Example of Creating Charts in Excel

In this tutorial, we'll build a basic column chart that shows the sold volumes against the sales year.

1. Start Excel
2. Fill in the blanks in the sample data table above. The below is how your workbook can now appear.

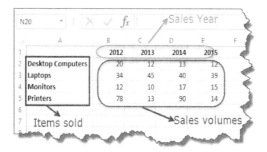

3. You can follow the steps below to get the desired chart type.

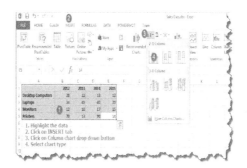

4. Choose the data you want to show in the graph.
5. Click on the INSERT tab from the ribbon.
6. Now click on the Column chart by dropping the down button.
7. Choose the type of chart you want.

16.2.1 Select Chart Type

Click the Insert button on the top banner until your data has been outlined in the Workbook. A segment with many chart choices is located around halfway down the toolbar. Recommended Charts are focused on prominence, but you can choose a different version by clicking either of the dropdown menus.

16.2.2 Create Your Chart

Click on the column chart icon from the INSERT tab and choose a clustered column.

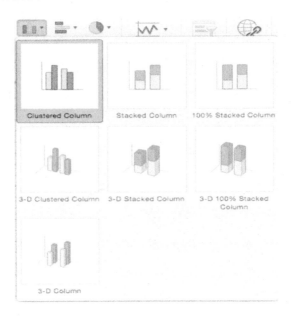

The chart will automatically appear in the center of the workbook from selected data.

Double click on the Chart Title and name your chart with the title.

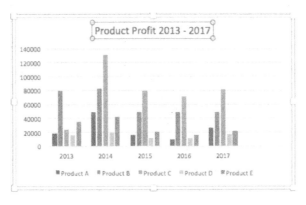

Chart Design and Format are the two sections on the toolbar you can use to make changes to your chart. Excel applies to style, layout, and format presets to charts and graphs by default; however, you can customize them by going through the tabs.

16.2.3 Add the Chart Elements

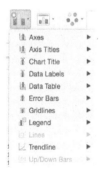

By adding chart elements to the graph or chart, you may improve it by clarifying details by adding meaning. Using the Add Chart Feature dropdown menu in the top left corner, you can choose a chart element (beneath the Home tab).

16.2.4 To Display or Hide Axes

Choose the axes. To view both horizontal and vertical axes on your chart, Excel will automatically pull the column and row headers from your chosen cell set.

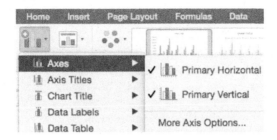

To delete the view axis from your chart, uncheck these choices. In this case, selecting Primary Horizontal will delete the year labels from your chart's horizontal axis.

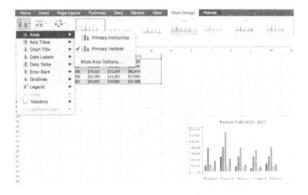

More Axis Options... opens a window with additional formatting and text options, such as inserting tick marks, labels, or numbers, or changing text color and height, from the Axes dropdown selection.

16.2.5 To Add Axis Titles

Select Axis Titles from the dropdown menu after clicking Add the Chart Element. Since axis names are not immediately added to charts in Excel, both Primary Horizontal and Primary Vertical would be unchecked.

A text box will appear on the chart when you press Primary Horizontal or Primary Vertical to generate axis names. In this case, we pressed both. Fill in the axis titles. We added the titles "Year" (horizontal) and "Profit" to this example (vertical).

16.2.6 To Remove or Move Chart Title

Select Chart Title from the Add the Chart Element drop-down menu.

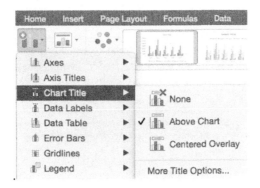

- To delete the chart title, click None.
- To put the title above the chart, click Above Chart. Excel can automatically put a chart title above the chart if you make one.
- To put the title inside the chart's gridlines, choose Centered Overlay. This alternative can be used with caution: you don't want the title to obscure any of your data or clutter your graph, as given below.

16.2.7 To Add Data Labels

Select Data Labels from the Add the Chart Element menu. For data marks, there are six options: None, Center, Inside End, Inside Base, Outside End, and More Data Labels are all options.

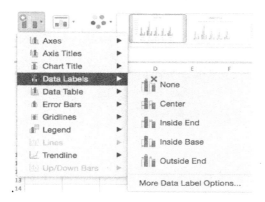

Each data point calculated in your chart would have a unique mark, thanks to the four placement choices. Select the desired alternative. If you have a limited number of details or a ton of extra room in your chart, this customization may be helpful. Adding data labels to a clustered column table, on the other hand, would undoubtedly appear cluttered. This is how choosing Center data labels looks, for example.

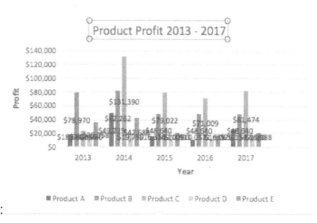

16.2.8 To Add a Data Table

Select Data Table from the Add the Chart Element drop-down menu. By pressing, you can use three pre-formatted choices as well as an extended menu.

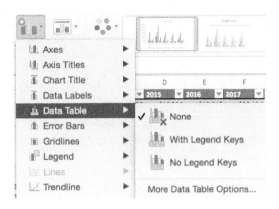

The default setting is None, which means the data table is not duplicated inside the chart.

Legend Keys shows the data set by displaying the data table under the list. The legend would be color-coded as well.

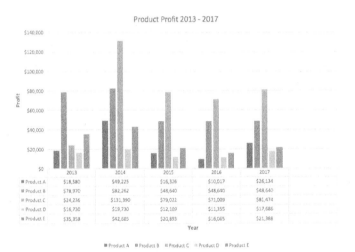

No Legend Keys also shows the data table under the chart but without the legend.

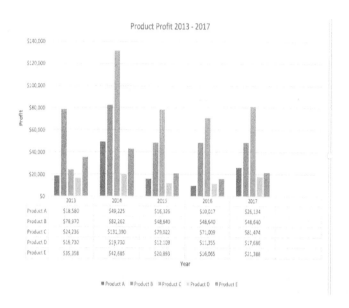

16.2.9 To Add Error Bars

Select Error Bars from the Add the Chart Element menu. There are four choices and More Error Bars Options: None (default), Standard Error, 5% (Percentage), and Standard Deviation. Using various standard equations for isolating error, error bars offer a visual representation of the possible error in the displayed results.

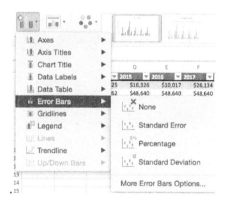

E.g., we click on "Standard Error" from the options, and we obtain a chart like the image below.

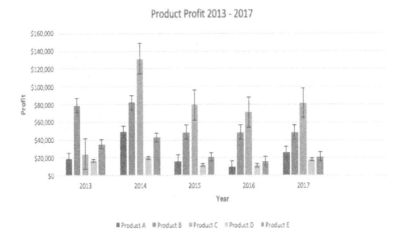

16.2.10 To Add Gridlines

Gridlines may be added to a chart by clicking Add the Chart Element and then Gridlines. There are four variations: Primary Major Horizontal, Primary Minor Horizontal, Primary Major Vertical, and Primary Minor Vertical, in addition to More Grid Line Options. Excel automatically adds Primary Major Horizontal gridlines to a column table.

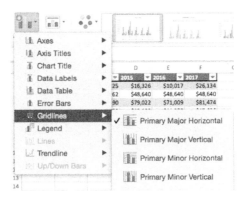

By pressing the choices, you can select as many different gridlines as you want. Here's what our chart appears when all four gridline choices are selected.

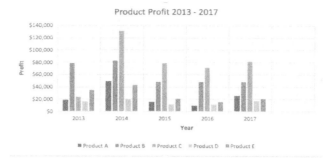

16.2.11 To Add a Legend

Select Legend from the Add the Chart Element drop-down menu. There are five legend positioning options and More Legend Preferences: None, Top, Left, Right, and Bottom.

The type and format of your chart will determine where the legend is placed. Select the alternative that appears to be the most appealing on your chart. When we press the Right legend placement, this is what our chart looks like.

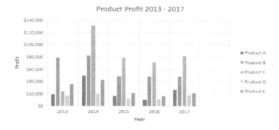

16.2.12 To Add a Trendline

Select Trendline from the Add the Chart Element drop-down menu. There are five choices: None (default), Linear, Linear Forecast, Exponential, and Moving Average, in addition to Further Trendline Options. Be sure you're using the right tool for your data collection. In this case, we'll choose Linear.

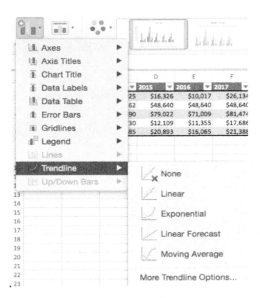

Excel provides a trendline for each commodity when we're evaluating five separate goods over time. Click Product A and then the blue OK button to build a linear trendline for it.

A dotted trendline will now appear on the chart to reflect Product A's linear progression. Linear (Product A) has now been applied to the legend in Excel.

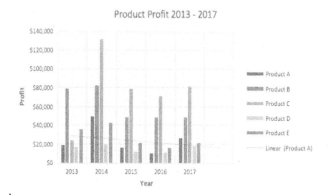

Double click on the trendline to show the trendline equation on the chart. The Format Trendline window opens on the right side of the screen. Select the box after the Display calculation on the chart at the base side of the screen. The equation will look like this:

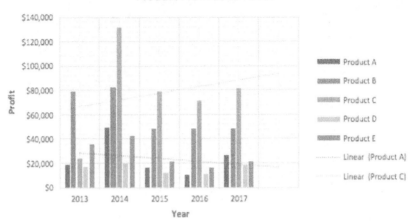

16.2.13 Adjust Quick Layout

Quick Layout is the toolbar's second dropdown menu, and it helps you easily adjust the layout of items in your chart (legend, titles, clusters, etc.).

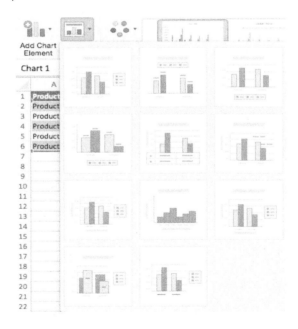

There are 11 simple interface choices to choose from. Hover your cursor over the various choices for a description, then choose the one you want to use.

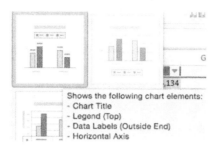

16.2.14 Change Colors

Change Colors is the next dropdown menu in the toolbar. Choose the color scheme that best suits your needs (these may be aesthetic or complement your brand's colors and theme).

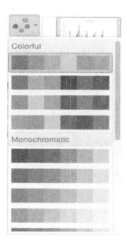

16.2.15 Change Style

There are 14 chart forms used for cluster column charts. The chart will be shown in Style 1 by design; however, you may adjust it to either of the other types. To see further choices, click the arrow to the right of the picture bar.

187

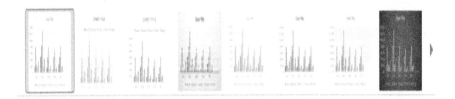

16.2.16 Switch Row/Column

To flip the axes, click the Switch Row/Column button on the toolbar.

Switch Row/Column

Switching the row and column, in this case, flips the product and year (profit remains on the y-axis). The chart is now organized by product (rather than by year), and the color-coded legend corresponds to the year (not product). To stop some doubt, go to the legend and shift the Series to Year's names.

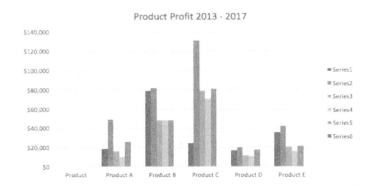

16.2.17 Select Data

This icon is for the change of range of your data.

Select Data

Click the OK button after you've typed in the cell set you like. The chart will refresh automatically to display the latest data set.

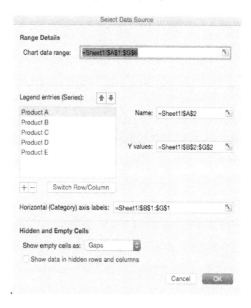

16.2.18 Change Chart Type

Choose from one of Excel's nine chart types to adjust the kind of chart you're working on. Of necessity, double-check that the data is suitable for the chart format you've chosen.

By pressing Save as Template..., you could also save your chart as a template.

You'll be presented with a dialogue box where you can give your template a name. For quick organizing, Excel can automatically generate a folder for your models. To save your work, click the blue Save icon.

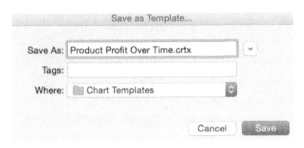

16.2.19 Move Chart

Move Chart

You'll see a dialogue box where you can pick where to put the chart. You may either use this chart to make a new layer (New sheet) or use it as an entity in another sheet (Object in). To continue, press the blue OK icon.

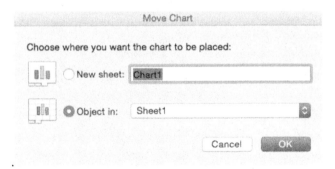

16.2.20 Change Formatting

You may adjust the colors, scale, design, fill, and orientation of all elements and text in the table, as well as insert shapes, using the Format tab. To make a chart representing your company's brand, go to the Format tab and use the shortcuts accessible (colors, images, etc.).

Select the chart element from the dropdown menu on the toolbar's top left hand.

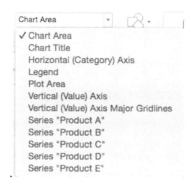

16.3 Top Five Excel Chart and Graph Best Practices

While Excel offers multiple styles and styling presets to improve the look and formatting of your table, using them does not guarantee that you can get the most out of it. The top five best practices for making your chart or graph as simple and practical as possible are outlined below:

1. **Clean it up:** Cluttered diagrams, such as those with many colors or text, are tough to interpret and don't stand out. Remove all distracting detail so that the viewers can concentrate on the argument you're attempting to make.
2. **Choose the right themes:** When choosing a theme, think about the audience, the subject, and the chart's key point. Though It's cool to try out various models, go for the one that better suits your needs.

3. **Use text carefully:** Charts and graphs are mainly visual aids, but you can almost certainly have some text (such as titles or axis labels). Be brief but precise, and be deliberate regarding the direction of every document (it isn't delightful to switch your head to read text written sideways on the x-axis, for example)
4. **Arrange elements wisely:** Think of where you want names, stories, icons, and other graphical elements to go. They can complement the graph rather than subtract from it.
5. **Arrange data before making the chart:** When people fail to sort their data or delete duplicates when making a chart, the image becomes unintuitive, leading to mistakes.

16.4 How to Enter Chart Data in Excel?

To create an Excel chart or graph, you must first supply Excel with data to work with. We'll teach you how to map data in Excel in this segment.

16.4.1 Step 1: Enter Data Into a Worksheet

1. Choose New Workbook from the File menu in Excel.
2. Fill in the information you intend to use to make a graph or chart. We're comparing the benefit of five separate items from 2013 to 2017 in this case. Be sure all the columns and rows have numbers. As a result, you'll be able to convert the data into a chart or graph with simple axis marks. This sample data is available for download below.

	A	B	C	D	E	F
1	Product	2013	2014	2015	2016	2017
2	Product A	$18,580	$49,225	$16,326	$10,017	$26,134
3	Product B	$78,970	$82,262	$48,640	$48,640	$48,640
4	Product C	$24,236	$131,390	$79,022	$71,009	$81,474
5	Product D	$16,730	$19,730	$12,109	$11,355	$17,686
6	Product E	$35,358	$42,685	$20,893	$16,065	$21,388
7						

16.4.2 Step 2: Select an Array to Create a Chart or a Graph From the Workbook Data

1. Click and move the cursor over the cells that hold the data you choose to include in your chart to highlight them.

2. Choose a chart form after the cell set has been illuminated in gray.

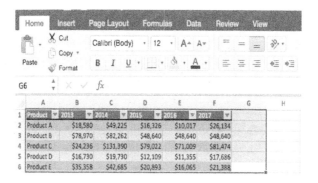

Chapter 17: Excel Table

Since your worksheet is arranged in rows and columns, you might mistakenly believe that the data is already in a chart. However, unless you expressly make it so, data in a tabular format is not a real "table."

A table in Excel is a unique entity that functions as a unit that helps you handle the table's contents independently of the rest of the worksheet results.

The screenshot below shows the difference between a standard set and a table format:

Range				Excel table			
Region	Jan	Feb	Mar	Region	Jan	Feb	Mar
East	$100	$150	$130	East	$100	$150	$130
West	$200	$260	$150	West	$200	$260	$150
South	$130	$160	$90	South	$130	$160	$90
North	$270	$250	$180	North	$270	$250	$180
Total	$700	$820	$550	Total	$700	$820	$550

On the other hand, an Excel chart is something more than a set of formatted data with headings. Within, you'll find a slew of useful features:

Excel tables are interactive by default, which means they extend and contract when you introduce and subtract rows and columns.

Visual filtering with slicers; integrated sort and filter choices.

Inbuilt table types make formatting a breeze.

When scrolling, column headings remain available.

Quick totals enable you to quickly sum and count data and find the average, minimum, and maximum values.

Calculated columns enable you to run a calculation in one cell to compute an entire column.

Calculations that are easy to decipher thanks to a specific notation that utilizes table and column names instead of cell references.

When you introduce or delete data from a table, dynamic charts change automatically.

17.1 How to Create a Table in Excel?

To convert several cells into a table, follow the steps below with the source data arranged in rows and columns:

1. Choose a cell from your data collection.
2. In the Tables group of the Insert page, select the Table button or use the Ctrl + T shortcut.
3. The Create Table dialog box appears, with all the details pre-selected; you can change the selection if necessary. Ensure the "My table has headers" is checked whether you choose the first row of data to become the table headers.
4. Choose OK.

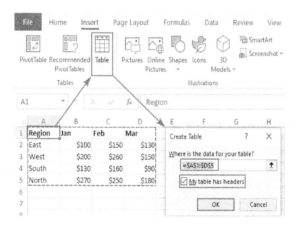

Therefore, Excel turns the data into a true table with the following default style:

	A	B	C	D
1	Region	Jan	Feb	Mar
2	East	$100	$150	$130
3	West	$200	$260	$150
4	South	$130	$160	$90
5	North	$270	$250	$180

17.1.1 Tips

- Before making a chart, clean and prepare the data by removing blank rows, giving each column a meaningful name, and ensuring that each row includes details regarding a single document.
- When you insert a table, Excel keeps all the existing formatting. To get the best performance, delete any original formatting, such as background colors, so it doesn't clash with the table theme.
- There is no limit on how many tables you can have per sheet; you can have as many as you like. Inserting at least one blank row and one blank column between a table and other details makes sense for greater readability.

17.2 How to Make a Table With a Selected Style?

The preceding example demonstrated the quickest method for creating a table in Excel, but it still utilizes the default style. Follow these measures to draw a table in the format of your choice:

1. Choose a cell from your data collection.
2. Choose Format as Table from the Styles group on the Home page.
3. Choose the theme you intend to use from the gallery.
4. Change the range if possible; in the Create Table dialog box, check the "My table has headers" box, and press OK.

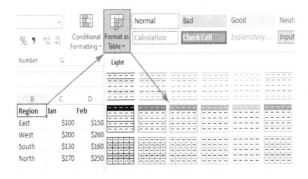

17.3 How to Name a Table in Excel?

When you create a table in Excel, it is given a defaulting name such as Table1, Table2, and so on. When working with several tables, modifying the default names to something more accurate and informative will simplify the work. Follow these steps to rename a table:

1. Choose a cell in the table that you want to work with.
2. In the Properties group of the Table Design page, choose the existing name in the Table Name box and replace it with a new name.

17.4 How to Use Tables in Excel?

Excel tables have many excellent features that make it easy to calculate, manipulate, and update data in your worksheets. Most of these options are simple and intuitive. A short rundown of the most critical ones can be found below. By contrast, auto-filtering is allowed for all tables. To filter the data in the table, do the following:

1. In the column header, click the drop-down arrow.
2. Uncheck the boxes next to the details you'd want to exclude from the filter. Alternatively, you should uncheck the box to deselect all the results, then check the boxes next to the data you wish to see.
3. If necessary, you can also use the Filter by Color and Text Filters choices.
4. Choose OK.

If you don't need the auto-filter function, uncheck the Filter Button box in the Table Style Options category on the Design tab to delete the arrows. You may also use the Ctrl + Shift + L shortcut to turn the filter keys on and off.

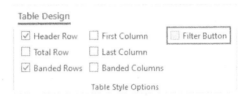

By adding a slicer to your table, you can also build a visual filter. To do so, go to the Table Design tab and choose Insert Slicer from the Tools group.

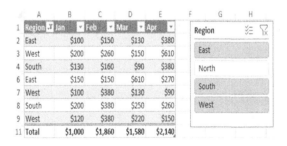

17.5 How to Sort a Table in Excel?

To sort a table by a particular column, simply select the appropriate sorting method from the drop-down arrow in the heading cell.

17.5.1 Excel Table Formulas

Excel uses a specific formula syntax called ordered references to calculate the table data. They have a host of benefits over traditional formulas:

- **They're simple to create.** Simply pick the table's data while creating a formula, and Excel will instantly build a detailed guide for you.
- **It's easy to learn.** Formulas are simpler to follow as structured references apply to table sections by name.
- **It is pre-filled.** Enter a formula in every cell to execute the same calculation in every row, and it will be replicated around the column.
- **Changed to its own.** When you amend a formula in one section, it affects all the other formulas in the same column.
- **Immediately updated.** Structured references update automatically as the table is resized or the columns are renamed.

17.6 How to Extend a Table in Excel?

When you type something in a cell next to it, the Excel table extends to accommodate the new details. When combined with formal sources, this automatically generates a complex spectrum for the formulas. Click Ctrl + Z if you don't want the latest data to be used in the chart. This would erase the table expansion while retaining the data you entered. A table may also be manually extended by sliding a small handle in the bottom-right corner.

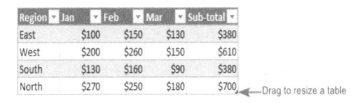

You may also use the Resize Table command to add and delete columns and rows. Here's how to do it:

1. Choose a location in your table by clicking somewhere on it.
2. In the Properties group of the Design tab, select Resize Table.
3. Click the range to be used in the table from the dialog box that emerges.
4. Choose OK.

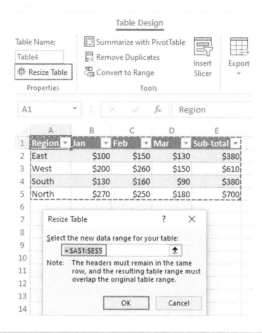

17.7 How to Change Table Style?

When you insert a table in Excel, it is immediately styled with the default theme. To modify a table's style, follow these steps:

1. Choose a cell in the table that you want to work with.
2. In the Table Styles group of the Design tab, choose the theme you choose to use. Click the Further button in the lower-right corner to show all the styles.

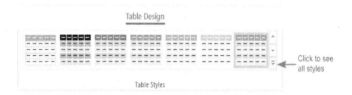

17.8 How to Remove the Table Formatting?

If you want all the features of the Excel table although none of the formatting, such as banded rows, table borders, and so on, you can do so by following these steps:

201

1. Click on every cell in your chart.
2. In the Table Styles group of the Design tab, press the More button in the bottom-right corner, then Clear under the table type models. Alternatively, choose None, the first style under Light.

17.9 How to Remove a Table in Excel?

It's just as easy to take out a table as it is to put one back. Simply do the following to convert a table back to a range:

1. Select Table> Convert to Range from the context menu of every cell in the table. Alternatively, on the Design page, in the Tools group, press the Convert to Range icon.
2. In the resulting dialog box, choose Yes.

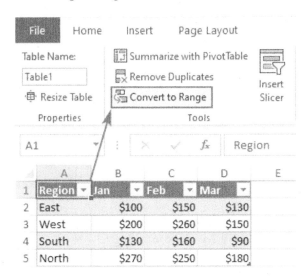

Chapter 18: How to Become a Data Analyst in 2022?

If you want to pursue a career in data science, take the following five steps:

1. Get a bachelor's degree in a discipline like math or computer science that emphasizes mathematical and analytical skills.
2. Acquire critical data analytics expertise.
3. Think of qualification.
4. Get the first job as a data analyst.
5. Get a master's degree in data science.

18.1 What Does a Data Analyst Do?

On a broad dataset, a data scientist gathers, processes, and conducts mathematical analysis. They learn how to use data to find answers to issues and solve problems. Data processing has progressed because of the advancement of computing and an ever-increasing shift toward technical intertwinement. The invention of the relational database breathed fresh life into data analysts, allowing them to access data from databases using SQL (pronounced "sequel" or "s-q-l").

Most data analytics positions include collecting and cleaning data to discover patterns and industry observations. The day-to-day duties of a data analyst vary based on the market, organization, or kind of data analytics you specialize in. Using market analytics tools,

Tableau, and scripting, data analysts may be responsible for developing dashboards, designing, and managing interaction databases and programs for various divisions within their organization.

Data analysts often collaborate with IT teams, management, and/or data scientists to assess operational priorities. They collect and clean data from primary and secondary sources and use standard statistical methods and techniques to evaluate and assess the information. In certain instances, they discover new prospects for the process of change by classifying trends, similarities, and patterns in varied data sets. Data analysts must also write updates on their results to inform essential stakeholders of the subsequent measures.

18.2 What Is Data Analytics?

Data analytics can be described as the method of extracting valuable insights from raw data by scrutiny. Your industry information, product advances, consumer dynamics, and so on are examples of such observations.

Data analytics is like putting together a jigsaw puzzle. The first step is to collect all the puzzle pieces and then correctly put them together to create the final image. In data analytics, you must analyze data from various sources, clean it, and then turn it into knowledge that humans can understand.

The information gathered may be organized, semi-structured, or unstructured. The end conclusion can be visualized as graphs and charts that show the analysis's exact findings. The research approach employs several methods and mechanisms.

Professionals that can assist companies in converting raw data into usable material, which can then aid in business development, are in high demand. In the world of data analytics, there are various work positions to choose from but being a data analyst is one of the most exciting. The next step is to learn how to become a data analyst. And Here's how you should do it.

18.3 Data Analyst Qualifications

Data analysts need these skills:

- **Programming languages like R/SAS:** Data specialists should be fluent in at least one programming language and have a functional knowledge of many others. For data collection, mathematical research, data cleaning, and data visualization, data analysts use programming languages including R and SAS.

- **Analytical and creative thinking:** Curiosity and imagination are essential characteristics of a successful data analyst. It's vital to have a solid understanding of mathematical methodology, but It's essential to approach challenges with a new and logical mindset. This will help the analyst generate outstanding analysis questions that will help the firm understand the subject better.
- **Effective communication:** Whether It's to a group of readers or a select group of executives making strategic choices, data analysts must accurately communicate their conclusions. The secret to performance is effective contact.
- **Computer visualization:** It requires a lot of trial and error to be good at data visualization. A good data analyst knows how to use different kinds of diagrams, scale visualizations, and which graphics to use based on the audience.
- **Back-end data warehousing:** Some data analysts work in this field. They build a data warehouse by connecting databases from various sources and searching for and managing data using querying languages.
- **SQL databases:** SQL databases are hierarchical relational databases. Data is contained in tables, and to do analysis, a data scientist pulls details from various tables.
- **Database querying languages:** SQL is the most popular querying language used by data analysts, with many derivatives such as PostgreSQL, T-SQL, and PL/SQL (Procedural Language/SQL).
- **Data mining, cleaning, and munging:** Data researchers must utilize other methods to gather unstructured data because it isn't conveniently placed in a folder. They clean and process the data until they have enough.
- **Advanced Microsoft Excel:** Data analysts should be comfortable with Microsoft Excel and be familiar with advanced modeling and analytics techniques.
- **Machine learning:** Data analysts skilled in machine learning are very useful, even though machine learning is not a required ability in most data analyst careers.

18.4 Data Analyst Responsibilities

The day-to-day activities of a data analysts are determined by where they work and the instruments they use. Any computer analysts favor mathematical tools and Excel over programming languages. Some researchers do regression analysis or generate data visualizations, depending on the challenges they're trying to solve. Data researchers with more experience are often referred to as "junior data scientists" or "data scientists in college." In specific scenarios, a data analyst/scientist may spend the morning writing queries or responding to standard requests and the afternoon developing custom solutions or playing with relational databases, Hadoop, or NoSQL.

"Creating prospect predictions for Fantasy Baseball is a huge part of my career. These determine the default rankings in our draft rooms and my preseason and in-season player rankings. Because our Fantasy product's readers and consumers depend on the precision of these predictions, It's critical to provide a solid statistical foundation for producing them. We have a lot of contact with our listeners throughout the season, and a big part of our job is to react to concerns regarding player importance and success. Whether produced by social networking channels, written and video material, or podcasts, these suggestions are based on statistical research." The following are some of a data analyst's most essential and planned responsibilities:

- **Understanding the goal:** A data analyst must first and foremost determine the organization's target. They must evaluate the available tools, comprehend the market problem, and gather the necessary information.

- **Querying:** To gather, store, manipulate, and extract data from relational databases such as MS SQL Server, Oracle DB, and MySQL, data analysts write detailed SQL queries and scripts.

- **Data mining:** Data is gathered from a variety of outlets and organized to extract new information. Data models are created as a result, and the system's reliability is improved.

- **Data cleansing:** A data analyst's primary responsibilities include data cleaning and wrangling. Initially, collected data is often sloppy and contains incomplete values. As a result, It's essential to clean the data gathered to prepare it for review.

- **Data examining:** For a logical examination of statistics, data analysts use analytical and mathematical methods, like programming languages.

- **Interpreting data trends:** Data analysts utilize various packages and repositories to spot developments and patterns in large databases, resulting in the discovery of previously unknown market insights.

- **Preparing summary reports:** Data analysts use data visualization software to create summary reports. These updates help the leadership team making informed choices on time.

- **Collaborating with other teams:** To ensure consistent execution of company criteria and identify process optimization opportunities, data analysts collaborate with the executive committee, production team, and data scientists.

18.5 What Tools Do Data Analysts Use?

Below are a few other practical techniques that data analysts use on the job:

- **Google Analytics (GA):** GA allows researchers to better analyze user details, such as patterns and aspects of consumer service that may be improved on landing pages or calls to action (CTAs)
- **Tableau:** Tableau is a data aggregation and analysis tool used by analysts. They will build dashboards and exchange them with other team members, as well as create visualizations.
- **The Jupyter Notebook System:** Jupyter notebooks render testing technology easy for data analysts. Because of its markdown functionality, non-skilled people enjoy the basic style of Jupyter notebooks.
- **Github:** Github is a forum for uploading and creating technical projects.
- **AWS S3:** AWS S3 is a cloud computing framework for data specialists who use object-oriented programming. Data scientists may use it to store and extract massive datasets.

18.6 Data Analysts Job

Today's data specialists must be compliant and adaptable. Analysts' jobs are becoming more complicated. Experienced researchers use predictive, and modeling analytics approaches to produce valuable observations and decisions. And they must justify what they've discovered to a group of perplexed laypersons. To put it another way, they would evolve from data analysts to data scientists.

According to new figures from the Bureau of Labor Statistics, market analysis analyst positions are expected to rise by 18 percent, while management analyst positions are expected to grow by 11 percent, which is far higher than the overall employment development. While data analysts can work in a comprehensive range of sectors, including banking, healthcare, information, professional services, engineering, and retail, technological advancements have developed in raising the analyst roles. We gather data at any level, and the organization of that data and the application of predictive analysis help society become a more incredible version of itself.

18.7 Data Analyst Salary

The amount of money you get is determined by your work duties. A senior data analyst with data scientist expertise will command a large fee. Data Analysts Earnings:

- Entry-level data analysts earn an average of $83,750 a year.
- Data analysts make an average of $100,250 a year.
- Senior data analysts earn an average of $118,750 to $142,500 a year.

18.8 Data Analyst Career Path

Data analysts are in high demand in nearly every industry. As a result, It's no wonder that demand for data analysts is expected to increase at a 19 percent annual pace over the next seven years. Since data processing is regarded as the most critical talent, any professional should study Data Science as soon as possible to advance in their careers. The following are several sectors with a vital requirement for data analysts:

Market Research: Data mining is seen as critical by 72 percent of advertisers to succeed in today's marketing environment. Data collection may be used to determine the effectiveness of marketing strategies. Companies may often utilize data mining to do consumer studies before introducing a new product or service.

Finance and Investments: Financial companies need both entry-level and specialist data analysts. The most popular job choice for data analysts at certain financial companies, such as investment banks, is management. Senior management will recommend you for advancement if you appear to be the strongest of your peers, and they see you as someone who can effectively handle recruits.

Revenue: Several data points related to product and service purchases are evaluated in a business, which aids in profits and consumer loyalty and identifying possible market obstacles. As a result, data analysts are required in this industry as well.

A data analyst fresher earns a good wage, which varies depending on his or her experience and ability set. Freshman skills can differ depending on the industry.

For example, a Data Analyst's usual task is to run queries against the available data to uncover interesting patterns and process data useful to Data Scientists. Data Analysts are primarily proficient in database query languages such as SQL. They can often compose scripts and create graphics based on the data they can better explain.

A Data Scientist, on the other hand, uses Machine Learning to build models. These models are used to create various forecasts and can often be used to describe the organization's future. When planning data for machine learning models, Data Scientists collaborate closely with Data Analysts. On the other hand, data scientists earn far more than Data Analysts due to solid demand and limited availability.

Many Data Analysts go on to become Data Scientists after gaining the required skills. Since Data Analysts also have specific essential expertise, the move to become a Data Scientist is not challenging. Many Data Analysts advance to the role of Data Scientist. A Data Analyst's job title is determined by the organization where he or she operates. However, as Data Analysts progress through the business hierarchy, their technological work becomes less important, and their administrative work becomes more critical. At a particular stage, promotion becomes more dependent on leadership and management abilities. As a result, Data Analysts must also develop their soft skills.

18.9 Is Data Analysis a Growing Field?

According to a McKinsey survey, there is a lack of 140,000-190,000 Data Analysts in the United States and 1.5 million Managers and Analysts who know how to utilize data analysis to guide decision-making.

IBM estimated that the number of positions for computer practitioners in the United States would rise from 364,000 to 2,720,000 by 2020 in its 2017 study The Quant Crunch: How the Need for Data Science Skills is Disrupting the

Labor Market. According to IBM, almost every one of the 2.8 million "analytically savvy" employees that will fill the void would have to leave occupations to do so.

Salaries have increased in tandem with demand, of course. According to Indeed, the annual wage for a Data Analyst in the United States is $68,523, with a Senior Data Analyst earning $86,500.

Junior Data Analysts are well compensated in some sectors. A Data Analyst working in natural resources and mining would expect to earn north of $100,000 on average, while those working in educational, scientific, and technological services can earn $90,000 on average, and Data Analysts working in finance and insurance can earn about $90,000 on average, according to a Springboard survey.

18.10 How to Become a Data Analyst With No Experience?

If you want to learn how to become a Data Analyst without any prior knowledge, the first move is to learn the necessary data skills, which you will then show publicly. Some of these abilities are simple to learn on their own, whereas others are more difficult. Even then, the area is vast and complex enough that deciding where to begin can be challenging. A formal learning experience that systematically addresses all the fundamentals is the perfect way to get started in the industry and guarantee that you understand what you still need to learn right away.

For example, Data Analytics courses and data science boot camps are common choices for aspiring Data Analysts. You will develop essential data skills and get hands-on experience in an accelerated learning format here, assurance that the time you spend learning is based on the fields where it would be most beneficial to you.

If you've mastered vital data skills, the next move of being a Data Analyst is to put them to use, preferably through creating your projects to post online. Posting the code, you've written, also as part of your coursework, on GitHub is a great place to show off your work—and your data skills. This will demonstrate your abilities and serve as the start of your professional portfolio.

Don't just stick to the basics. When interviewing for a Data Analyst position, a creative, well-executed data assignment that you complete on your own is a perfect opportunity to show your data skills and attract new hiring managers. Choose a subject that you're passionate about, pose a query about it, and try to address it with details. Document your path and provide your conclusions with a concise overview of your methodology, showcasing your analytical data knowledge and imagination.

Finally, joining an online data science group like Kaggle can be a perfect way to prove that you're involved in the community, demonstrate your skills as a budding Data Analyst, and begin to expand your knowledge and scope.

Chapter 19: What Skills Should You Look for While Hiring an Excel Expert?

Microsoft Excel is a software tool created by Microsoft that several companies utilize to simplify everyday operations such as employee data management, financial data management, debit sheet management, data collection, and more. As a result, this extremely user-friendly platform is commonly utilized in divisions ranging from human resources to sales, communications, and data analytics, among others. Expertise levels can range from beginner to advance.

As a recruiter, you would evaluate applicants for their excel abilities based on the work criteria. However, do you know what skills to search for? Let's look at each case individually, from simple to specialized Excel abilities and work role-based Excel experience.

19.1 For Entry Level/Administrative Jobs

Many managerial positions and entry-level career profiles require simple MS Excel skills to complete time-consuming and routine activities.

The below is a compilation of Microsoft Excel skills to search for while recruiting entry-level employees:

- SUMIF/SUMIFS
- COUNTIF / COUNTIFS
- Filters for data
- Sorting of data
- Pivot Tables
- Formatting of cells
- Validation of data
- Excel keyboard shortcuts

- Worksheets
- Page Layout Management
- Charts and their interpretation

To evaluate all the above abilities, you can ask applicants application-based questions to test their basic Excel competence. It will offer you a good understanding of how they will tackle real-life challenges in a matter of minutes.

19.2 For Senior Level/Excel Specialists/Excel Experts

Excel calculates, evaluates, and gets fruitful outcomes for complicated questions using advanced functions, algorithms, and VBA programming, even though it is primarily a data management method. An advanced degree of Excel knowledge is needed for job positions that include data science, data processing, programming, or project management responsibilities.

- Excel Worksheets
- INDEX + MATCH
- Functions
- Advanced Formulae
- Advanced Charting
- VLOOKUP
- PIVOT Tables & PIVOT Reporting
- VBA & Macros
- Conditional Formatting
- Tool Bars

You can hire:

- Bookkeeper
- VBA Projects Developer
- Office Manager
- Accountant
- Project Manager

19.3 Business Analyst Excel Skills

A market analyst acts as a liaison between the organization's IT department and business stakeholders. Almost all the roles of a market analyst involve developing the approach, designing enterprise infrastructure, defining project criteria or priorities, finding potential markets, and optimizing their business. A business analyst must have hands-on experience with simple to advanced Excel functions and their functionalities to accomplish any of these KPIs. You must have skills like:

- Pivot Tables
- VLOOKUP
- SUMPRODUCT
- SUMIFS, COUNTIFS
- MATCH
- IFERROR
- Charts and Chart Analysis
- INDIRECT
- IF Function
- Merge Data
- MACROS
- Histograms
- Conditional Formatting
- Data Validation
- Regression
- Data Analysis

19.4 Data Analyst Excel Skills

Data researchers are constantly tinkering with data to extract particularly relevant market knowledge that can be used to make smarter, more informed business decisions. Their primary responsibility is to assess market danger, collect data, and determine what is detrimental to the company. You must have skills of checklist like:

- Pivot Tables
- Macros
- LOOKUP Functions
- Cross Reference Table
- Data Filters
- Flat Data Tables
- Advanced Charts
- Graphics Data
- Data Interpretation
- Number Series
- Operators

- Worksheet

19.5 Auditor Excel Skills

An auditor oversees preparing and conducting investigations, as well as reviewing financial statements. He maintains that the documents are clear of bugs and that taxes are paid on schedule. As a result, they would review financial records, build audit test documentation, audit work-papers, and so on. You must look for:

- Internal Audit of Inventories
- Balance Sheet Audit
- Internal Auditing
- Charts
- Worksheet
- Functions
- Operators
- Pivot Tables
- Macros
- Conditional formatting
- VLOOKUP, HLOOKUP

You can hire:

- Internal Auditor
- Audit Clerk
- Auditor Associate

19.6 Seven Tips to Improve Basic MS Excel Skills

19.6.1 Master the Shortcuts

You will save a lot of time by learning specific keyboard shortcuts. Even if most machine and Internet users nowadays couldn't imagine navigating online without a click or at the very least a touchpad, using just the keyboard can save you a lot of time. Using Ctrl+C and Ctrl+V to copy and paste is typically second nature to you. Ctrl+Z to reverse the previous operation, Ctrl+PgUp to move between worksheet windows, Ctrl+A to select the whole worksheet, Ctrl+F to locate objects, & Ctrl+K to add hyperlinks are several other helpful shortcuts. Microsoft has compiled a comprehensive collection of Excel keyboard shortcuts.

19.6.2 Import Data From a Website

It's also crucial to learn how to import data because it will significantly speed up the workflow. If you come across a website with a lot of data that you think could be useful for one of your ventures, you can transform it into a worksheet by going to File > Import External Data and then pressing New Web Query. When you press this button, a new window appears with your browser's homepage highlighted, and the page's URL highlighted. Copy and paste the path to the website you want to view into the Address box. Click OK, and you're done! Your information is entered into an Excel spreadsheet.

19.6.3 Filter your Results

If you have a big spreadsheet with a lot of data, the best thing you can do is use the Auto filtering function. Select Data > Filter > Auto filter to do so. Using one of the small boxes, you can filter the results to meet your specific requirements.

19.6.4 Calculate the Sum

If you use Excel often, using shortcuts to measure the sum of an entire column or set of cells will save you a lot of time. Once you've picked the first empty cell in the list, use the shortcut Alt + = rather than manually enter the formula (the one located at the end of the numbers). After you've run this order, click Tab to see the response in Excel.

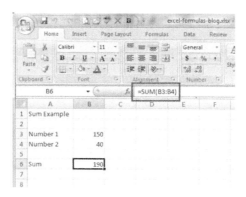

19.6.5 AutoCorrect and AutoFill

You can learn how to type less in Excel if you want to save any more time. This can be done in two ways: AutoFill and AutoCorrect. AutoFill saves you time, mainly when manually typing in a numbered list. Go to the Edit tab, point to Fill, and then press Series to unlock it. AutoCorrect is a function that corrects misspelled words & typos automatically. To allow AutoCorrect, go to the Tools tab and pick AutoCorrect from the drop-down menu.

19.6.6 Display Formulas

You can switch between Excel's usual regular monitor and the display mode, which shows you how the formulas look in the method, with only a single keystroke. Ctrl + is the formula. When you press this combination once in a spreadsheet, Excel can display formulas rather than the output of these formulas.

19.6.7 Manage Page Layout

You'll need to know how to handle page layout if you want your printouts to appear as impressive as the view onscreen. These choices can be found by going to the Page Layout tab. Consider experimenting with page numbering, columns, and page boundaries to see how they function before expanding.

Conclusion

The new Excel models provide all you need to get started and become a specialist, including a variety of great functionality. MS Excel recognizes patterns and organizes data to save you time. Create spreadsheets easily from templates or scratch, then perform calculations with modern features.

It's both simple and advanced applications that can be used in almost every business environment. The Excel database allows you to create quickly and easily, view, edit, and share data with others. When reading and editing excel files attached to emails, you will create spreadsheets, data tables, data reports, budgets, and more. As you've become more acquainted with different concepts, you can know the new resources and functionality that Excel provides to its users. The truth is that with Excel features, you can meet almost every person or company requirement. What you need to do is invest your time and expand your knowledge. The learning curve for improving your skills will be long, but you may find that items become second nature with experience and time. After all, a man becomes better through practice.

Everything you must do to make your life easier—and potentially impress others in your office—is to master these fundamental Excel skills. But bear in mind that no matter how experienced you are with this versatile tool, there is still something new to discover. Whatever you do, continue to keep improving your Excel skills—it will help you not only keep track of your own money but it may also contribute to a better career opportunity in the future.

YOUR GIFT

I want to show my appreciation by **offering** the **PDF version** of the book <u>with all images</u> and the **Best Ready-to-Use Excel Templates** to improve your productivity.

Please click the following link to get the gifts or scan the QR Code:

GIVE ME MY GIFTS

Thanks

Thank you so much for reading my book.

I really can't tell you how much it means to me that somebody chose to read something I created.

<u>I hope you enjoyed it as much as I enjoyed writing it.</u>

It took a lot of time, energy and hard work to write the best possible result for your experience, which is why it would mean a LOT if you could **take just two minutes** from your day and **leave a review on Amazon**. It doesn't have to belong or be detailed - any comment will do.

Scan the QR Code and follow the simple instructions from there on!

If there's anything from the book that you didn't understand or have any suggestions to improve the book, don't hesitate to contact me at the email address mysuggestionbook@gmail.com and I will make sure to respond as soon as possible.

Many thanks for considering my request.

Printed in Great Britain
by Amazon